THE
CABIN CREW
INTERVIEW MADE EASY

The complete interview blueprint
and workbook

The Cabin Crew Aircademy presents

THE CABIN CREW INTERVIEW MADE EASY WORKBOOK

First Edition by Caitlyn Rogers

ISBN: 978-1-908300-50-8

Printed in the United Kingdom
10 9 8 7 6 5 4 3 2 1

Copyright © 2017 Caitlyn Rogers
All rights reserved.

Library of Congress Cataloging-in-Publication Data

COVER PHOTOGRAPHY CREDITS

Photographer: Andrey Yakovlev
Art Director: Tat'yana Safronova
Model: Marina Azarova
Style, Makeup: Lili Aleeva
Hair Style: Ovo Arakelyan

© CC- BY-ND 2012 Andrey Yakovlev & Lili Aleeva

With special thanks to AeroFlot Airlines®

Published by:

THE CABIN CREW
INTERVIEW MADE EASY

DISCLAIMER

This book is designed to provide information and guidance on attending a cabin crew assessment. It is sold with the understanding that the author is not engaged in rendering legal or other professional services. Such topics, as discussed herein are for example or illustrative purposes only. If expert assistance is required the services of a competent professional should be sought where you can explore the unique aspects of your situation and can receive specific advice tailored to your circumstances.

It is not the purpose of this guide to reprint all the information that is otherwise available but instead to complement, amplify and supplement other texts. You are urged to read all the available material, learn as much as possible about the role and interview techniques and tailor the information to your individual needs.

Every effort has been made to make this guide as complete and accurate as possible, however, this guide contains information that is current only up to the printing date. Interview processes are frequently updated and are often subject to differing interpretations, therefore, there are no absolutes and this text should be used only as a general guide and not as the ultimate source of information.

All information in this book is offered as an opinion of the author and should be taken as such and used with discretion by the reader. You are solely responsible for your use of this book. Neither the publisher nor the author explicitly or implicitly promises that readers will find employment because of anything written or implied here.

The purpose of this guide is to educate and inform. The author shall have neither liability nor responsibility to you or anyone else because of any information contained in or left out of this book.

The views and opinions expressed within this guide are those of the author and do not represent the views of any of the airlines mentioned within. This book is neither associated, approved, affiliated with, nor endorsed by any such Airlines.

WELCOME

Hello and welcome to
The Cabin Crew Interview Made Easy

It's great to have you here and I'm so pleased to be part of your journey. I'm also super excited for you, because you have now taken the first step to realising your dream of becoming cabin crew. Woo hoo.

Now, are you ready to bag yourself the job?
Great. Then let's get started

It's time for your career to take flight...

CONTENTS

GETTING STARTED — page 10

STEP ONE : RESEARCH — page 17

STEP TWO : APPLY — page 63

STEP THREE : PREPARE — page 159

STEP FOUR : ATTEND — page 179

STEP FIVE : CONCLUDE — page 249

CAITLYN ROGERS

There was a time where I felt broken by the interview process. I had been attending interviews unsuccessfully for several years, and was coming to the end of my rope. My confidence was battered, and every setback hit me harder and harder.

In 2003, I attended an interview that was especially difficult. Anxiety was out of control, and I walked out before any of the tasks begun because I felt so depleted.

Once I arrived home, instead of becoming sad, I got angry. In this angered state I vowed never to attend another interview unless I was 100% prepared to nail it.

Getting angry was the best thing that could have happened, because it made me strong. Strong enough that I was able to look back upon my previous interview experiences with an objective point of view for the first time. A point of view that enabled me to make postive changes to myself and my approach.

I spent almost 2 years researching and preparing before I ever attended another interview. I left no stone unturned in my determination to succeed. Thankfully that effort and time paid off. My first two applications to CrossAir and Emirates were both successful and I subsequently took the position with Emirates.

Since that time, I have continued my research into the hiring practices of each airline and compiled everything I have learnt into this book for you to use for yourself so that you don't have to spend two years researching as I did.

All the guidance I provide is tried and tested by myself and my readers, who have found their own success with various airlines. Now in it's 6th edition, this guide is up to date with current processes and I hope it helps you achieve your dream career too. No doubt you deserve to live your dreams and I wish you all the very best.

5 STEPS TO SUCCESS

This book is all about action and, within the following pages, you will find a clear and effective blueprint to follow - a blueprint that will take you through the entire interview process in a 5 step sequence.

STEP 1	RESEARCH
STEP 2	APPLY
STEP 3	PREPARE
STEP 4	ATTEND
STEP 5	CONCLUDE

Each aspect of the application and selection process is covered in detail, right through to the conclusion.

GETTING STARTED

There are two ways you could work thorugh this course for maximum return on your investment:

Step by Step

If you have the time or are new to the cabin crew recruitment process, I recommend working through each section in the order they are presented, completing each task as you progress.

Since there are some areas that are easily overlooked, this will give you the most bang for your buck, ensuring you have all the information you need and are fully prepared..

Dip in & Dip out

Short on time? Then feel free to dip in and out as needed. This approach also works well if you have specific areas of concern that you want to address directly.

How much time do you need?

Naturally, the more time you can put into this course, the more you will get out of it, however, the goal isn't to make you an interview expert (heck that's my job). The goal is to get you out there living your dream, and in the shortest time possible.

So, only you can be the judge of how much time is needed. This may be as little as one week, or it could be as much as 60 days.

But, if you take action, **you will get results.**

KEY TAKEAWAYS

#1 Schedule it

Schedule an hour a day (or several hour chunks throughout the week) to go through the modules. Make yourself, your career and this course a priority. You'll be thankful you did.

#2 Commit to taking action

I've compiled the data for you, so all you need to do is take action. **You've got this !!!**

Ideally you should allow one month or more to prepare. This will allow you ample time to study the material thoroughly, and apply the strategies without feeling too rushed.

However, it's not always the case that you will have this luxury of time. So, what's the best way to prepare when you only have a matter of weeks, or less?

Step #1 Prepare your application materials

Photographs are a requirement for most airlines, so you should have these readily available.

Although you will be filling out an application form, I highly recommend drafting up your CV as well. This will help you fill out your application form and give you a clear breakdown of your history to refer to.

Step #2 Read what's relevant to your circumstances

If you struggle with any element in particular, maybe your confidence holds you back or you struggle to form cohesive answers, put effort into developing those areas.

STEP #3 Gather facts about the airline

When you are rushed for time, it is tempting to skip the research section of this course, however, it would be a cardinal sin to arrive at the interview without having at least a basic knowledge of the airline's operations. Having background knowledge about the airline will show that you are enthusiastic and prepared. A quality often desired in cabin crew.

STEP #4 : Prepare for potential questions

At the very least, you should be prepared to answer questions such as:

- » Why do you want to become cabin crew?
- » Why do you want to work for us?
- » Why should we hire you?
- » What are your weaknesses?

Also be sure to gather a selection of examples which demonstrate your customer service and teamworking experience., particularly those of an adverse nature.

STEP #5 : Prepare a list of questions

Having intelligent questions prepared for the recruiters will set you apart as a prepared and enthusiastic candidate.

STEP #6 : Rehearse

Rehearsing the interview process under simulated conditions will highlight potential areas of weakness. This will give you a better idea of where to focus your time and energy.

STEP #7 : Prepare your outfit

This may seem obvious, but you'd be surprised how many people leave this step until the morning of the interview only to find that they don't have anything appropriate to wear, or have stains on their attire. Your groomng is important for the cabin crew role, so make a good impression by planning your attire ahead of time.

STEP #8

Do the best you can

Once you have all the above steps completed, try to get as much reading in as possible. The average reading speed is said to be 150-250 words per minute. This means that, even at the slower pace of 150 words, you'll be able to get through much of the content with a few hours set aside. Do the best you can.

Remember, if you don't sacrifice for what you want, what you want becomes the sacrifice, so put your all into making this a success and you'll reap the rewards.

STEP #9

Believe in yourself

When you have been through a few cabin crew interview experiences, it is easy to feel overwhelmed by the process, but I assure you that it's not complicated or tricky. All you need is some guidance and strategies, and that's what I will provide you with in this step by step blueprint. It's time to realise your cabin crew dreams.

> "
> Choose a career you *love*
> and you will never work a day
> in your life
>
> *Dare to dream* ✈

STEP ONE
RESEARCH

so you can stand out as an informed applicant and bag the job of your dreams

WELCOME

Welcome to step one and congratulations on taking an important step towards your future. It's great to have you on the program.

I hope you are excited!!! I am certainly excited for you because **together we are going to make some serious progress towards your cabin crew dream.**

So, let's waste no time and get this ball rolling... **Welcome to Step One of** The Interview Blueprint and the all important topic of **Research**.

UGH, WAKE ME WHEN IT'S OVER...

Ugh, I know what you must be thinking, research is boring and mundane. Do I really have to do this?

Before you skip ahead or run away to the nearest Costa (oh wait, that's me), please bear with me a few moments and I will attempt to change your mind.

HERE'S THE DEAL...

Do you know how many people turn up to an interview not knowing a single thing about the airline? Other than it's list of exotic destinations! Well, I can tell you that it's well above 90%, and that's being generous.

But more surprising than that, do you know how many people actually arrive to an assessment only to be turned away because they failed to meet the basic requirements? Well, I'm glad to say that this one does have far better statistics, but it does and needn't happen.

WHAT THIS MEANS...

This means, If you spend just a small amount of time with this module, not only will you arrive with the certainty that you do actually qualify for the position, but you are also going to **stand out** as someone who has taken the time to do their homework. And this my dear friend is exactly the type of person that the airline is looking to recruit.

Even better, though you'll fly through your ab-initio training because you'll be leaps and bounds ahead of everyone else who is still catching up with the basics. It's a total win-win.

Now, doesn't that sound like it's worth sticking around for?

Because you have commited to purchasing this coursebook, I already know you are a doer. So, what do you say? Are you ready to bag that job?

Great, let's get started...

MODULE OUTLINE

This module is split into three distinct sections, these are:

> **Section 1: Research the recruitment profile**

Do you know what airlines are seeking? Within this section we will take a look at what airlines look for in their potential cabin crew, also known as The Person Specification. Here we will look at the eligibility, suitablility and the specific requirements.

> **Section 2: Research the airline**

Next we will take a look at the airline so that you can arrive armed with facts and solid reasons to justify your answers and demonstrate your enthusiasm.

> **Section 3: Research the corporate culture**

Finally we'll delve into the corporate culture. This is the heart of the airline and where a mis-match could make or break your outcome.

THE AIRLINE RECRUITMENT PROFILE

You can download supplementary FREE bonuses by visiting
www.cabincrewaircademy.com/bonus

THE PERSON SPECIFICATION

For the employment of cabin crew, airlines consider three key elements, these are:

ELIGIBILITY

SUITABILITY

SPECIFIC REQUIREMENTS

Together, these three elements form a **'person specification'**.

This person specification is referred to throughout the selection process to determine each candidates suitability for the position.

Over the coming pages, we'll take a look at each of these in order.

ELIGIBILITY

Eligibility are the basic requirements which must be met in all circumstances. They are mostly based on facts and are likely to include any of the following:

> Passport and/or visa requirements
> Level of education
> Previous experience
> Language abilities
> Physical profile

Each airline's eligibility criteria will be different to some degree, and can change according to the airline's ongoing needs. Be sure to complete the action step in the workbook before you apply.

SUITABILITY

Unlike eligibility, which is based on facts, suitability is based on **'Core Competencies'** and are determined by observation.

Core competencies are a collection of personal qualities, skills, knowledge and experience that are necessary for optimal performance in the job.

While there are several desirable characteristics for cabin crew, there are four fundamental core competencies, these include:

- Ability to work within and as part of a **team**
- A strong focus on **customer service**
- The ability to **communicate** well and at various levels
- **Resilience** and the ability to remain calm in adverse conditions

SPECIFIC REQUIREMENTS

Following the eligibility and suitability requirements, airlines proceed to customise their requirements according to their specific standards and requirements.

These standards and requirements cover several criteria, and are subject to ongoing revision. For example:

> **Swimming abilities**
> Some airlines have strict swimming requirements. This can range from a basic minimum distance to more advanced capabilities such as treading water and pulling someone to safety.

> **Previous cabin crew experience**
> A new airline may view previous cabin crew experience as a prime requisite during its start up stages, while a prestigious and well established airline may have no distinct preference.

> **Medical experience**
> If the airline determines that there is a shortage of crew with medical experience, skills within the medical field may be valued more highly.

> **Language ability**
> If the airline extends its route network, a particular language fluency may become highly desirable.

DIFFERENT OUTCOMES

While performance is an obvious factor, the different and changing considerations which make up the person specification explain why it is possible to be rejected by one airline, but accepted by another, or unsuccessful on one attempt, and then successful at the next.

We will examine these requirements in further detail when we visit your worksheets. First we will take a deeper look behind each of the elements.

PHYSICAL PROFILE

Due to the general physical nature of the job, airlines have stringent health and fitness guidelines in place for its cabin crew. While each airline will have its own requirements, the following guidelines will highlight the most common criteria.

HEALTH & FITNESS

As glamorous as the job may seem, your health will be affected by the lack of routine, climatic and time zone changes, and long working hours so good health and a strong immune system is essential for dealing with these conditions.

You will also need a good overall level of fitness for dealing with the general physical nature of the job, which includes opening and closing heavy emergency doors and standing for long periods.

When offered the position, you'll go through a **vigorous health screening**, so, if you do have any ongoing medical concerns, you'll want to determine if those are managable and won't interfere with your employment. I'd also recommend minimising sick days at work and uneccessary trips to the doctor as these records will be requested as part of the pre-employment process.

As a general aside, you'll also do well to maintain your physical fitness with regular exercise and consuming a healthy and balanced diet. This is not a vanity requirement as is often misunderstood.

Civil Aviation Authority

The Civil Aviation Authority Guidelines

Officially, the Civil Aviation Authority (CAA) has outlined the following health guidelines for cabin crew:

» Free from any physical or mental illness which might lead to incapacitation or inability to perform cabin crew duties
» Normal cardio respiratory function
» Normal central nervous system
» Adequate visual acuity 6/9 with or without glasses
» Adequate hearing
» Normal function of ear, nose and throat

* This information is correct at the time of printing.

HEIGHT

Airlines have very strict height requirements. These height restrictions have been put in place because a very short person may have difficulties reaching the overhead compartments or opening the emergency doors. Conversely, a very tall person may struggle within the cramped environment.

Height ranges vary from airline to airline, however, you can expect a typical minimum height of between:

5'2" (158cm) and **6'2" (188cm)**

Decompress your spine and grow up to 2" taller

As we age and during the course of our day, gravity causes our spines to compress.. By stretching out daily, it is possible to increase your height by as much as 2 inches.

The length of time it will take, and the amount of height you will gain does vary. This method is not a guaranteed fix but, if you are only slightly below the height restriction, stretching out and hanging from a pull up bar could make a difference for you.

REACH

Over recent years, aircraft configurations have changed and airlines have started to introduce reach requirements in place of or in addition to it's height requirements.

A reach requirement simply requires the ability to reach necessary components inside the aircraft which are typically between:

6" (182cm) and **6'10" (212cm)**

For some airlines, the reach test will only involve a simple line on the wall that you reach up and touch. However, there are airlines, such as British Airways, who have stricter tests that involve grabbing and turning a handle without shoes and without rising onto your tip toes.

Important guidance concerning reach tests

Please be sure to carry out your own reach test at home before you apply to your chosen airline. I cannot stress this enough. Although you may fit comfortably within the height range, if you have shorter arms, you may fail this test and the airlines will make no exceptions.

If you are a close call, measure on the morning of your interview and keep up your stretching routine every day.

AGE

Employment regulations generally prohibit discrimination on the grounds of age so it is improbable that you will encounter an upper age limit beyond the mandatory retirement age and it is not uncommon to find working cabin crew members that are well into their 40's and 50's.

Lower age limits do apply due in large part to the selling of alcoholic beverages. While there is no set standard within the industry, it is typically between 18 and 21 years.

Age discrimination

Discrimination does happen in the airline industry, just as it does in any industry, and I have provided additional guidelines to help you to avoid this in the companion guide entitled **The Inside Scoop.**

You can download this FREE guide by visiting www.cabincrewaircademy.com/bonus

APPEARANCE

It is a myth that airlines only hire candidates who embody perfect figures and harbour model looks, however, there is no denying that airlines do favour candidates who are well groomed and portray a polished image.

If you look through the recruitment information for the airline you wish to work for, you will find the requirements are clearly laid out, but, in general, most airlines prohibit the following:

NO FACIAL PIERCINGS

NO VISIBLE TATTOOS

NO CRAZY HAIR COLOURS

NO OUTRAGEOUS HAIR STYLES

Fresh and simple is the way to go

WEIGHT

While weight is an avenue that is certainly open to discrimination, particularly for those who fall within the higher end of the spectrum, it is unlikely to be a problem if your weight falls within normal parameters.

Airlines often refer to a BMI chart for this purpose, so you can determine your own proportions, by referring to the BMI chart below.

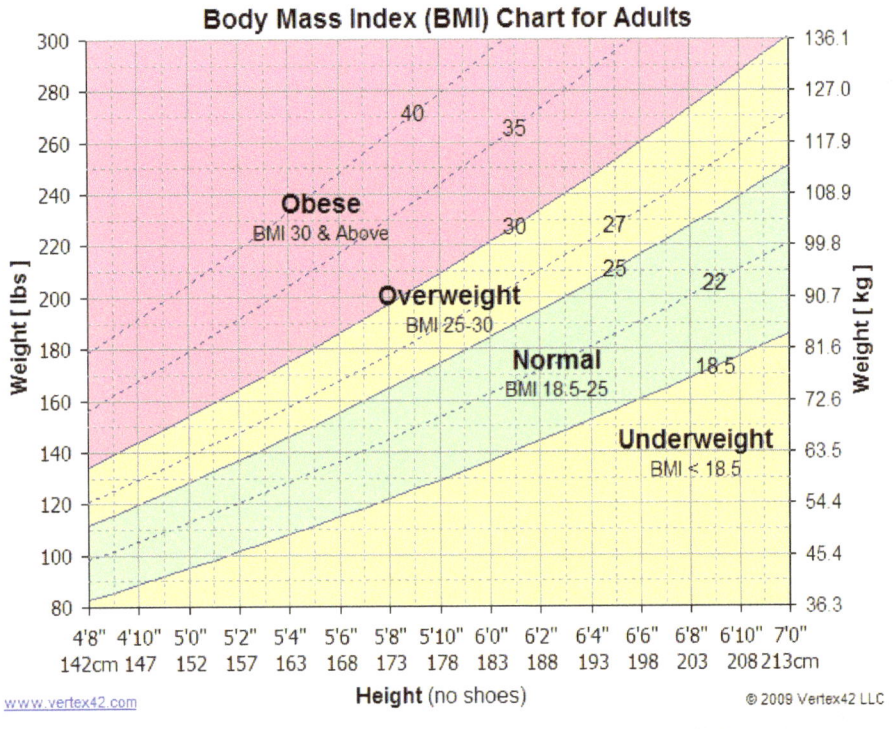

Accuracy note

If the majority of your body mass is made up of muscle, this chart will provide inaccurate results. This chart is used for guidance only and your physical structure will be observed.

ACTION STEP

Cabin Crew Research
The Requirements

AIRLINE:

Navigate to your selected airline's website, and begin to check yourself against the person specifications listed

- [ ] Passport, visa and residency *(if noted)*
- [ ] Min/max age restrictions
- [ ] Min/max height restrictions
- [ ] Reach requirements
- [ ] Level of education
- [ ] Languages spoken
- [ ] Swimming abilities
- [ ] Customer service experience
- [ ] Min/max height restritctions
- [ ] Medical experience / qualifications
- [ ] Previous cabin crew experience
- [ ] Other requirements

FURTHER RESEARCH

Next, take a look through the airline literatiure and begin to extract any key competencies that the airline use. This could be the way they describe their active crew, or it could be desired characteristics of the applicants they are seeking to employ. You may need to do some rummaging for this.

Noted core competencies?

As an example, Emirates specifiy the following: Professional, Empathetic, Progressive, Visionary, Cosmopolitan, while Cathay Pacific specify polished interpersonal skills, a positive attitude and a customer-oriented mindset British Airways value resilient, flexible, creative professionals with an unrelenting commitment to customer satisfaction.

virgin atlantic

At Virgin Atlantic, we want our customers' experience of flying with us to be as memorable as the adventure that awaits them when they land. So what do we look for in our future Cabin Crew? We want true customer champions who put our customers at the heart of everything they do. Working as part of a cohesive and dynamic team you'll balance your passion for customer care with your ability to maintain the highest of safety and security standards at all times.

Our crew are amazing ambassadors for lots of reasons. They're resilient, friendly, collaborative, proactive, supportive and caring. But everyone brings their own unique quality to the role. Our fabulous Crew come from all walks of life so you don't need to have previous Cabin Crew experience to apply.

http://careersuk.virgin-atlantic.com/customer-services/cabin-crew [Accessed 26 Apr. 2017]

BRITISH AIRWAYS Careers

A real team player, you're passionate about people and driven to delight every customer. Crucially, you're always ready to adapt to change and innovation. Whether you're responding to changing conditions mid-flight or trying out a brand new service, you'll put customers' interests first. Your enthusiasm for creating great experiences means you're totally engaged with everything from health and safety to our products and services.

Jhttps://jobs.ba.com/jobs/intheair/cabincrew/ [Accessed 26 Apr. 2017]

Emirates Group Careers

Are you dynamic and passionate, friendly and empathetic? The Emirates Cabin Crew team is a cosmopolitan mix of young professionals from over 140 countries that collectively speak more than 60 languages.

They are innovative forward-thinkers, travel-hungry explorers who tirelessly exceed customer expectations across 120 destinations over 6 continents on the latest Emirates aircraft. It's what makes Emirates Cabin Crew unique and a critical part of the Emirates award-winning team, honoured time and again for service excellence.

http://emiratesgroupcareers.com/english/careers_overview/cabin_crew/default.aspx [Accessed 26 Apr. 2017]

American Airlines

Our Flight attendants are the face of American Airlines and are service professionals of the highest caliber, with a desire, drive and passion to provide outstanding service. As we work to restore American Airlines to the greatest airline in the world, it's you, your ability to develop relationships and your ability to take care of our customers that makes the difference. Our customer's experience is a reflection of your experience as an employee. We're committed to making your experience great so you can do the same for our customers. Flying is more than what we do... it's who we are.

https://jobs.aa.com/go/Flight-Attendants/2537300/ [Accessed 26 Apr. 2017]

QANTAS

Our Flight Attendants are the face of Qantas - taking what's best about Australia's lifestyle, attitude and people, and sharing it with the rest of the world. They're known for their absolute commitment to safety, genuine and engaging service, and confidence in dealing with a variety of situations - including emergencies.

http://www.qantas.com/travel/airlines/flight-attendants/global/en [Accessed 26 Apr. 2017].

PUTTING IT TO GOOD USE

Now that you have compiled the data, it's time to put it to good use. If there are two things I'd like you to take away from this section, it is these two distinct take away tasks:

> **Measure up**

Measure yourself up against the height and reach requirements. Even if you are tall enough to pass the height marker with ease, please still carry out a reach test because these can be decieving if you have shorter arms. Always be safe and test. If you are close, measure on the day and keep stretching.

> **Use the specific competencies**

If the airline has injected any specific competencies within it's recruitment literature, whether this is how they describe their crew or the desired characteristics of the applicant, you can be sure they value these qualities very highly. So guess what you are going to do with those? That's right, you are going to inject those exact key words and any similar meanings, throughout your answers and your resume. We'll cover this in more detail in future modules.

RESEARCH THE AIRLINE

SECTION OBJECTIVES

As you conduct the research within this module, your own reasons for wanting to join the airline will likely be enhanced. This means that when the recruiter asks you a question such as "Why do you want to work for this airline?" or "Why should we hire you?" you are going to be armed with facts and solid reasons to justify your response and demonstrate your enthusiasm.

This will achieve the two objectives of this section, which are:

> To have you standing out as an informed applicant.

> To enable you to effectively demonstrate your fit for the airline

YOU'LL DISCOVER

So here's what you will discover within this module:

> **Where to look**
> I will show you some hidden gems that will make your research tasks quick, accurate and up to date.

> **What to learn**
> You will learn how much and to what depth is necessary, thereby only learning what is essential and helpful to your candidacy.

WHERE TO LOOK

Social media pages are the first place to check for up to date information about the airline that is fresh off the press, however, for the purposes of recruitment, you'll want to dig a little deeper.

The best place to get up to date, accurate and comprehensive information about an airline, it's past, present and future, is in it's **press pack**, also known as a **media kit**.

The press pack is a comprehensive, yet condensed set of promotional materials that have been put together for members of the media. Essentially, this is the equivalent of a resume but for the airline. You can find such packs by visiting the airline's website. Keep a look out for **Press or Media Centre,** typically located at the footer of the page.

Also keep a look out for **press releases** or **important news** within the same section of the website, as these will contain up to date information or initiatives that may be too recent to have been included within the press pack.

Another great source for the basic information is Wikipedia, however, the information may not be completely up to date, so it is best consulted for historical facts only.

virgin atlantic

Here is an example taken from the Virgin Atlantic website
www.virgin-atlantic.com

The link followed from the media centre takes you to the page below.

Helpful links

- About us
- Conditions of carriage
- Customer service
- Accessibility
- The Virgin Atlantic Blog
- Sustainability
- Canadian tariffs
- Want a career?
- Contact us
- Media Centre ←
- Mobile app
- FAQs

Media Centre

Here's what we've been up to…

Press releases
Check out our latest press releases here.
› Press releases

Virgin Atlantic directors
Read more about our decision makers.
› Virgin Atlantic directors

Worldwide media centre teams
Contact details for our media centres.
› Worldwide media centre teams

Press kit
Take a look at our press kit.
› Press kit

Our media library
Download media files including videos, imagery and audio files.
› Check out our media library

Want to know more?
Why not browse our website and see what we offer our customers?
› Virgin Atlantic website

Investor relations
Find out more about our business performance
› Our 2014 annual report (PDF - 4.3mb)
› Our 2015 annual report (PDF - 4.6mb)

QUICK TIP

Can't find the link?

If you canët find the link on the website, go to good old Google and type in (name of the airline) press kit

This will bring up a list of matches that will take you directly to the area you need to go.

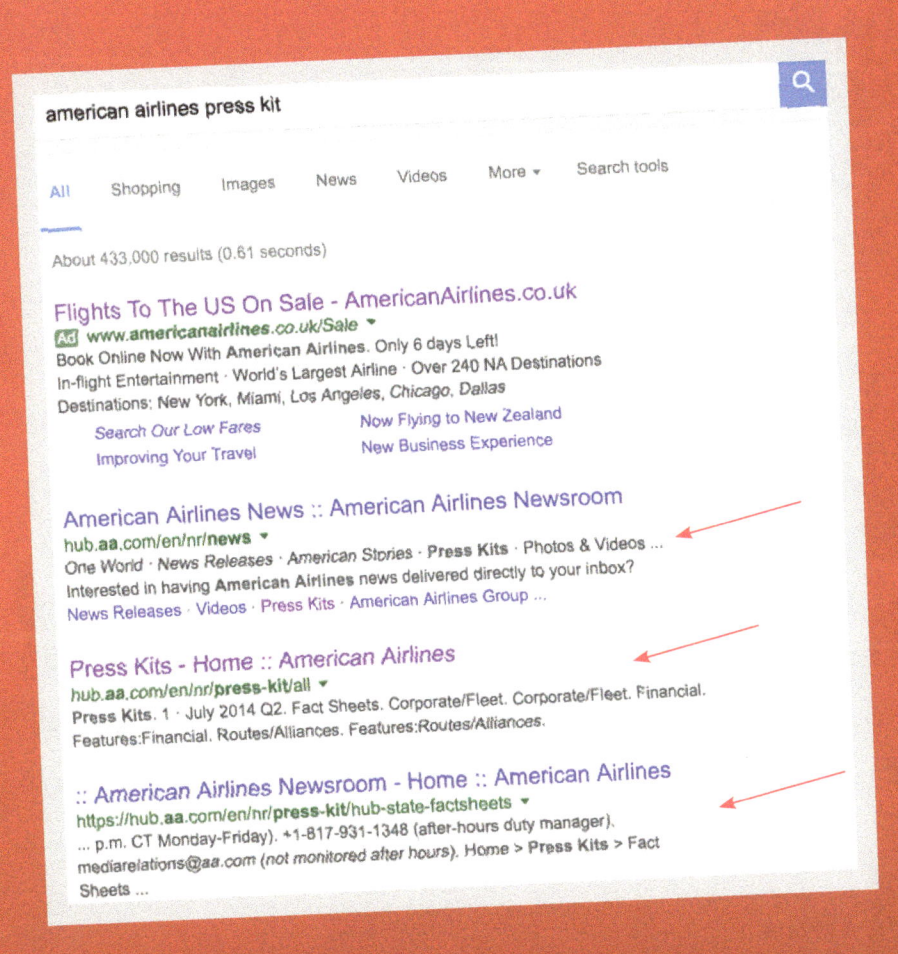

WHAT'S IN THE PACK?

A press kit will typically contain the following elements:

- Overview of the airline
- Profiles of key people
- Route and aircraft information
- Important news coverage
- Awards and initiatives
- Mission, goals & objectives
- Alliances

and many more interesting facts and goodies...

WHAT TO LEARN

You will find there is a tonne of information in these press packs, and you certainly do not need or want to know all of it. So, you will need to sift through and extract just a few key bits and pieces. Here are some things to look out for:

- Who is the key person? (e.g. CEO, founder or chairman)
- Is the airline part of an alliance? Or does it have any partnerships?
- What are the important growth plans? (1 year, 5 year, long term)
- What are three of the most prominent awards? How many have they won? What does the airline pride itself on?
- What is the story behind it's incorporation? When did it begin operations?
- Which 3 airlines are considered to be the closest major competitors? What are key differences?
- What is the frequent flyer programme called?
- How many destinations are in their route network? Does it focus on a particular region? Do they have plans to change or add to this?
- Is there anything significant about their fleet of aircraft? How many? What type? Does it have plans for updating its fleet?
- What is the overall mission of the airline? What is it's tagline?
- Is there anything unique or distinctive about this airline?

Although this list may appear overwhelming at first, you'll be surprised how much of the information you will retain just by extracting and then writing it out in your workbook.

The bottom line is, these are all the facts about your dream airline, and future employer. It's worth learning about

ACTION STEP

Airline Research Fundamentals

AIRLINE:

Tagline or Overall Mission

IATA Code   *(e.g. EK for Emirates)*   Date Founded

Key People   *(e.g. CEO, Chairman, or Founder)*

Hub/Main Operating Bases

Frequent Flyer Program

Alliances or Partnerships

Fleet Size

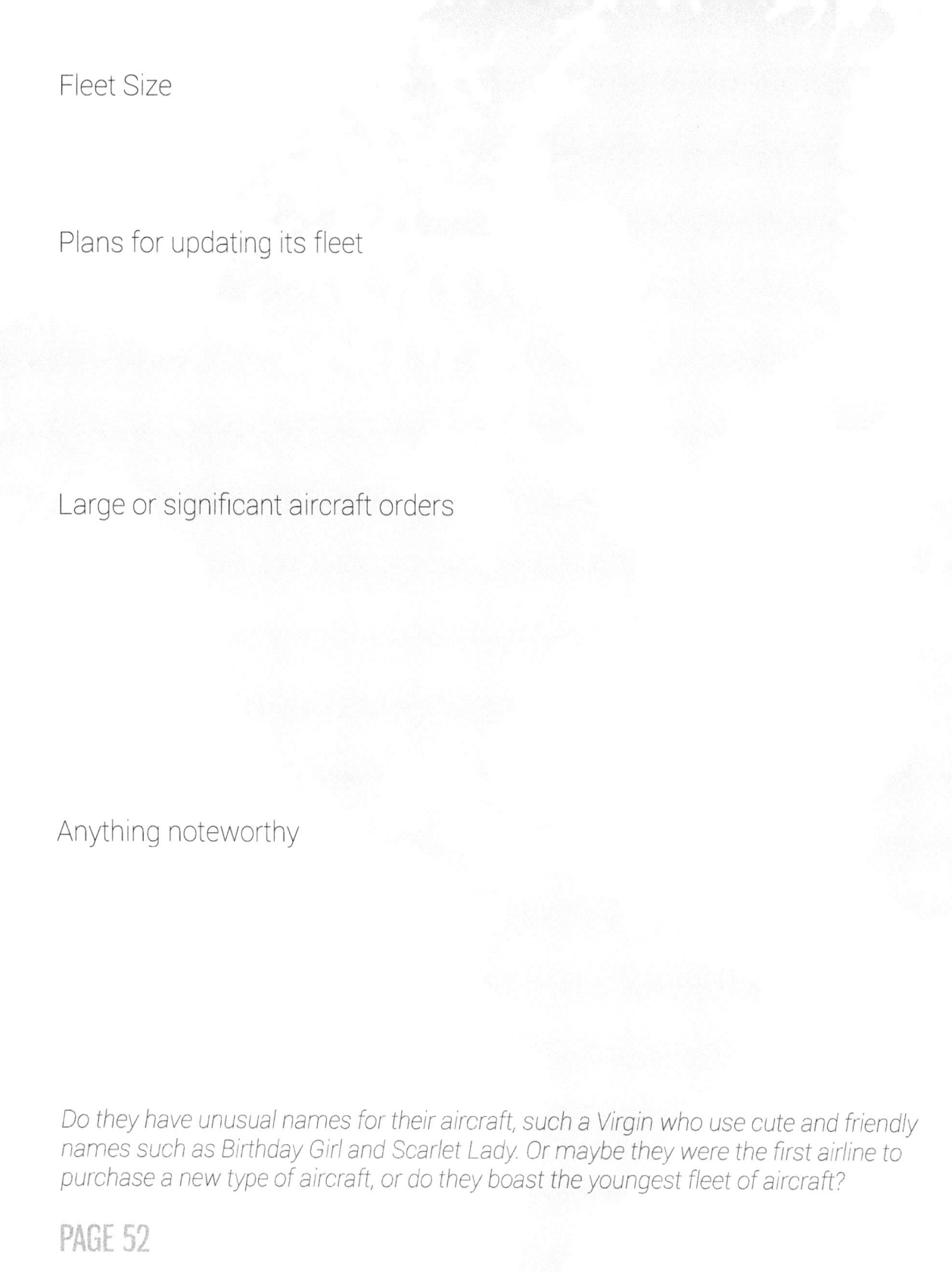

Plans for updating its fleet

Large or significant aircraft orders

Anything noteworthy

Do they have unusual names for their aircraft, such a Virgin who use cute and friendly names such as Birthday Girl and Scarlet Lady. Or maybe they were the first airline to purchase a new type of aircraft, or do they boast the youngest fleet of aircraft?

How many destinations?

Does it focus on any particular region?

Plans to change or add to their network

Anything noteworthy

Is the airline the first to fly to a particular destination? Has the airline carried more passengers to a particular destination than any other?

How many awards won?

What are three of their most prominent awards?

Of particular interest are Airline of the year and those related to customer service

What does the airline pride itself on?

Anything noteworthy

Has the airline won a particular award for several years in a row? Have they picked up an award that is highly significant?

Short term growth plans

Medium term growth plans

Long term growth plans

Who are the three closest competitors?

How do they differ in their operations?

Any other notes?

PAGE 58

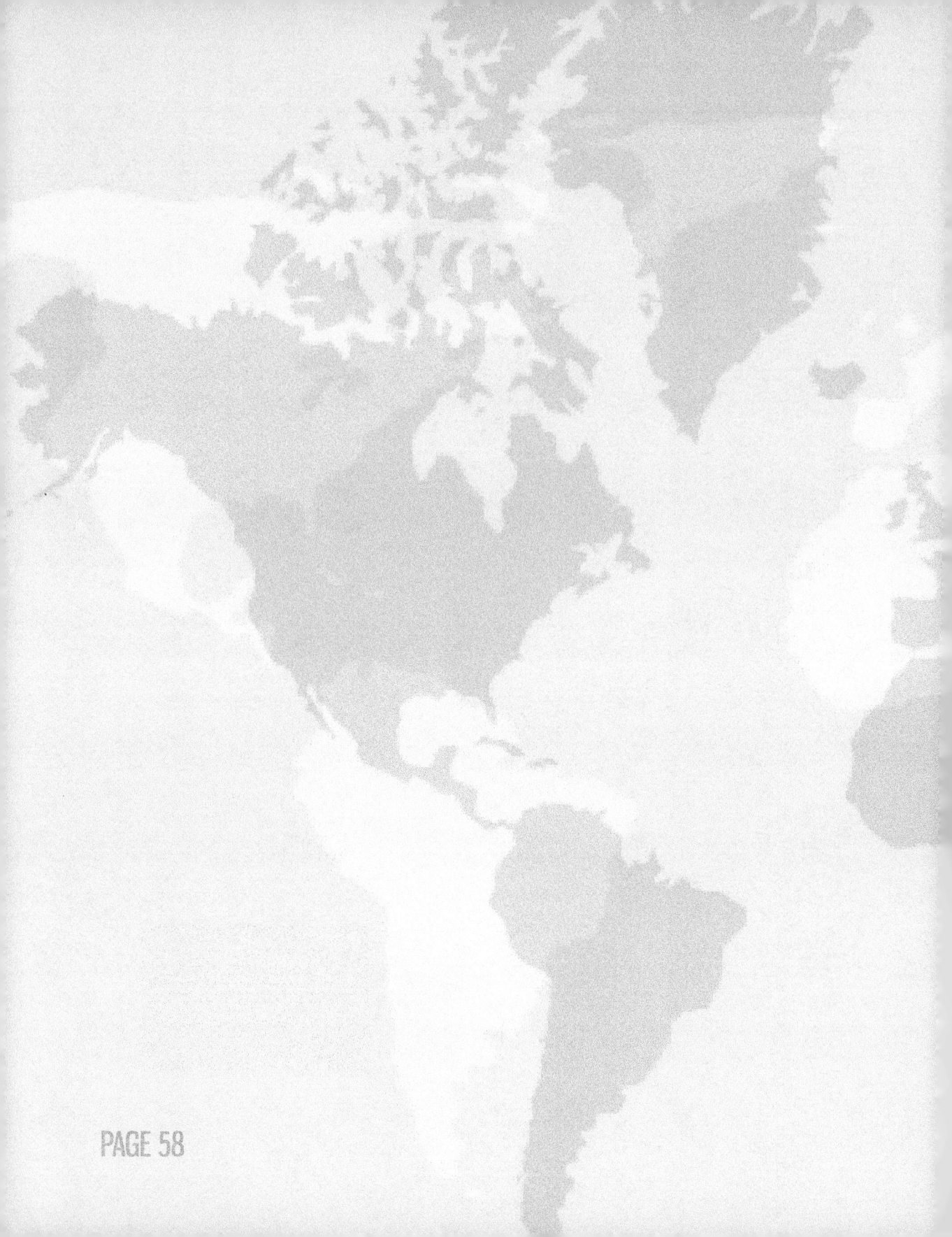

ASSESS THE CORPORATE CULTURE

THE DECIDING FACTOR

Corporate culture is a term used to describe the collective attitudes, beliefs, behaviours and values that exist within an organisation. In essence, it is the character of the airline. This aspect is so important, it is often the deciding factor as to whether certain candidates are successful or not.

Imagine, for example, a candidate who is rather introverted and values a very formal approach. Such a candidate would likely feel out of place with an airline such as Southwest or Virgin Atlantic who are very down to earth and value a fun service, but may fit right in with a professional carrier such as Emirates.

This is not to say that one is right and the other is wrong, it's all about fit. Getting the right fit is not only vital for the airline, but also vital for you if you are to be happy long term.

During the cabin crew assessment process, you will be constantly observed according to this culture and if your personality doesn't appear to fit, it is unlikely you'll be successful in the interview process. No matter how well you perform or what skills you have. As such, you need to be very clear about what this corporate culture is and whether you feel you really would be happy within it.

This is the very reason airlines conduct group interviews the way they do, it's an easy way to gauge your personality.

AIRLINE:

Describe the corporate culture

AIRLINE:

Describe the corporate culture

WOO HOO

That's a wrap for Module 1: Research and you are now armed with some **valuable** information.

As you progress through the book, you will make good use of the information you have compiled. For now, take a break, grab a Costa or whatever you fancy and come back when you are ready to start on Step 2 where you'll start to put together your application pack.

You are officially more informed than 90% of candidates who attend a cabin crew interview.

Congratulations.

STEP TWO
APPLY

Time to take action and apply for your dream job

WELCOME TO STEP TWO

This is an exciting module because we're going to delve into the application process.

This program is all about taking **ACTION**, so we begin this module with a massive action step to get the ball rolling and that is filling out the application form. There are two potential outcomes for this module, these are:

OUTCOME 1
Apply for the position

If you have an airline in your sights and qualify for the role now, by the end of this module you are going to submit your application. WOO

OUTCOME 2
Be ready to apply for the position

If, for any reason, you aren't ready to apply just yet, you will have the application ready for when that time does come.

Whichever outcome is right for you at this time, you are going to come away from this module prepared with a **killer application**.

STEP 1 : Compile your résumé / CV
Having a powerful resume will serve you well throughout the entire process. Within this step you'll create one that's perfect for you and your background

STEP 2 : Produce your photographs
Photographs are an essential element for any airline application, and some airlines will have very strict requirements about their presentation.

STEP 4 : Complete the application form
With the data gathered and application materials produced, now comes the exciting part. First we will examine typical questions and look at the most effective way to appraoch them, and then you will transfer your data into an actual application form that will be ready for submission.

STEP 6 : Submit the application form *(Optional)*
By this step, you have a compelling and powerful application kit ready to submit to your chosen airline. Whoop whoop.

YOUR RESUME/CV

WELCOME

Within this section, we'll take a look at refreshing your resume, also referred to as a CV or curriculum vitae.

You may not need to submit your resume to the aiirline, but it is useful for quick reference. In addition, there are some airlines who have a resume handover session as part of their open day. This session can be very quick and brutal, with many candidates getting cut from the process early based on a quick skim of the resume. You'll need a resume that has immediate appeal if you are to make it through this phase.

But don't worry, by the of this section, you"ll have a storng resume, full of your accomplishments and skills that will be transferrable to your airline application and stand out during a handover.

KEY POINTS

Your résumé is a very powerful document because it represents the best you have to offer. To make this document even more powerful, we are going to take a look at the following three areas.

FORMAT **OUTLINE** **OPTIMISE**

FORMAT

Depending on your career path to date, you'll want to pick a format that will highlight your strengths and minimise any areas of percieved weakness. The three basic formats are:

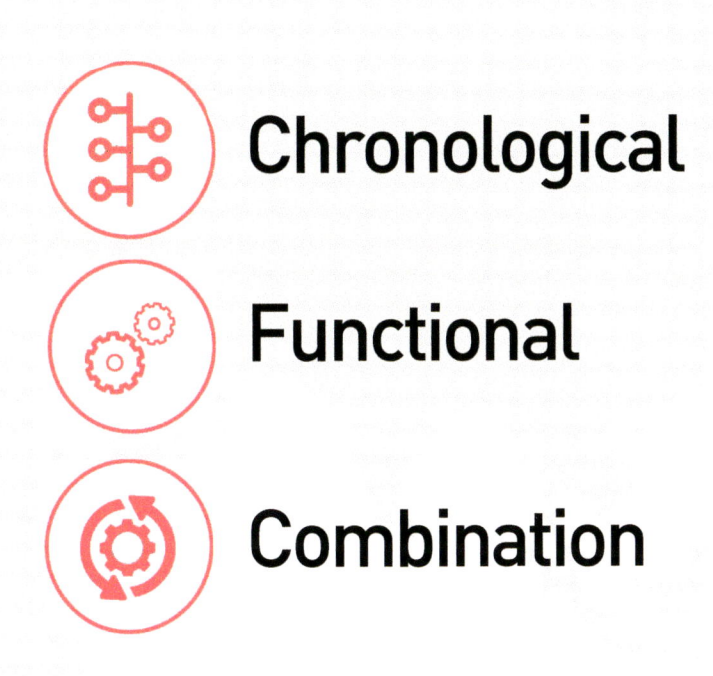

- **Chronological**
- **Functional**
- **Combination**

CHRONOLOGICAL

The chronological résumé highlights the dates, places of employment and job titles, having employment and education detailed first.

IDEAL FOR

» Demonstrating career progression
» If you want to highlight your career within the airline industry

AVOID IF

» You have large gaps in employment or a chequered history
» Are going through a major career change

Here is a typical outline of a chronological format:

> Personal Information
> Career Summary
> **Detailed Career History**
> (In Reverse Chronological Order) ← **DEFINING SECTION**
> Additional Skills & Achievements
> Education & Qualifications
> Interests & Hobbies
> References

The focus with this format is on your career history, so you will display the employer, date from and to, job title and a breakdown of your responsibilities starting from the most recent first.

FUNCTIONAL

A functional résumé focuses on skills and achievements and uses functional headings, such as Sales, Customer Service and Teamwork, instead of the chronological employment data.

IDEAL FOR

- Downplaying an extreme career change
- Concealing large gaps in employment or a chequered employment history.
- To highlight a relevent skill set

AVOID IF

- You are a recent graduate or are lacking experience
- You lack relevant or transferable skills

Here is a typical outline of a functional format:

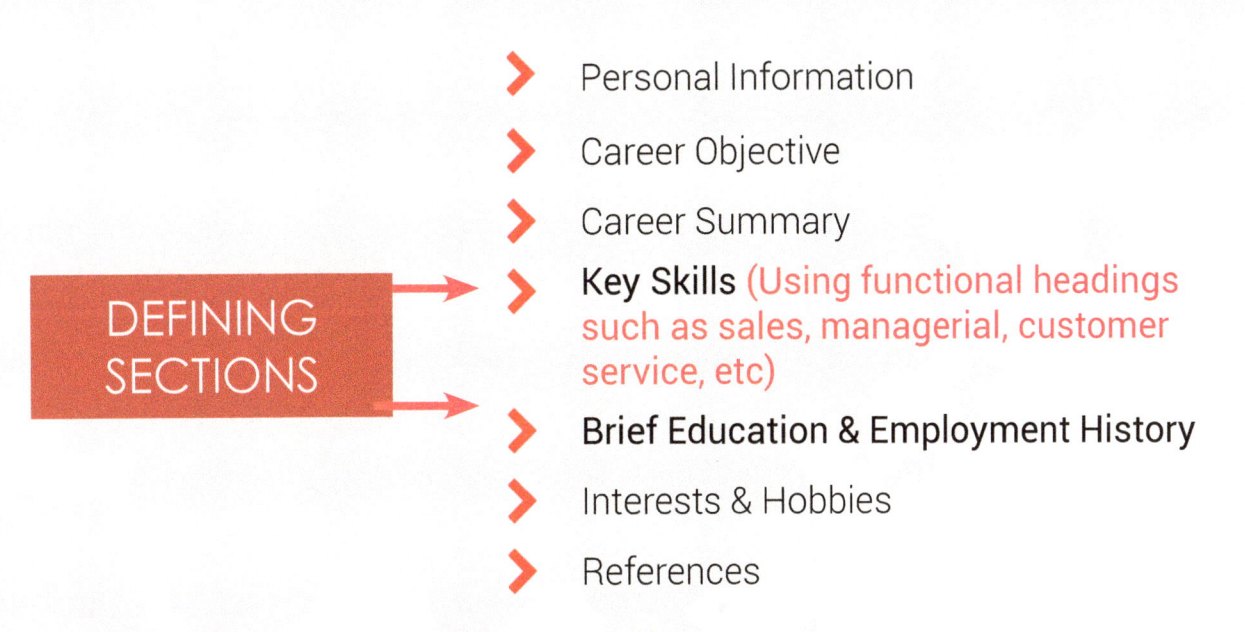

- Personal Information
- Career Objective
- Career Summary
- **Key Skills** (Using functional headings such as sales, managerial, customer service, etc)
- **Brief Education & Employment History**
- Interests & Hobbies
- References

DEFINING SECTIONS → Key Skills, Brief Education & Employment History

The format focuses more on key skills, so break those down into strong areas of interest to the airline, and elaborate on how these have been demonstrated. Rather than a detailed breakdown of your career and education, you will want to include just a brief overview.

COMBINATION

The combination résumé, is a combination of the chronological and functional formats.

IDEAL FOR

» Showcasing a relevant and developed skill set
» Making a career change
» Highlighting lots of relevant expertise

Here is a typical outline of a combination format:

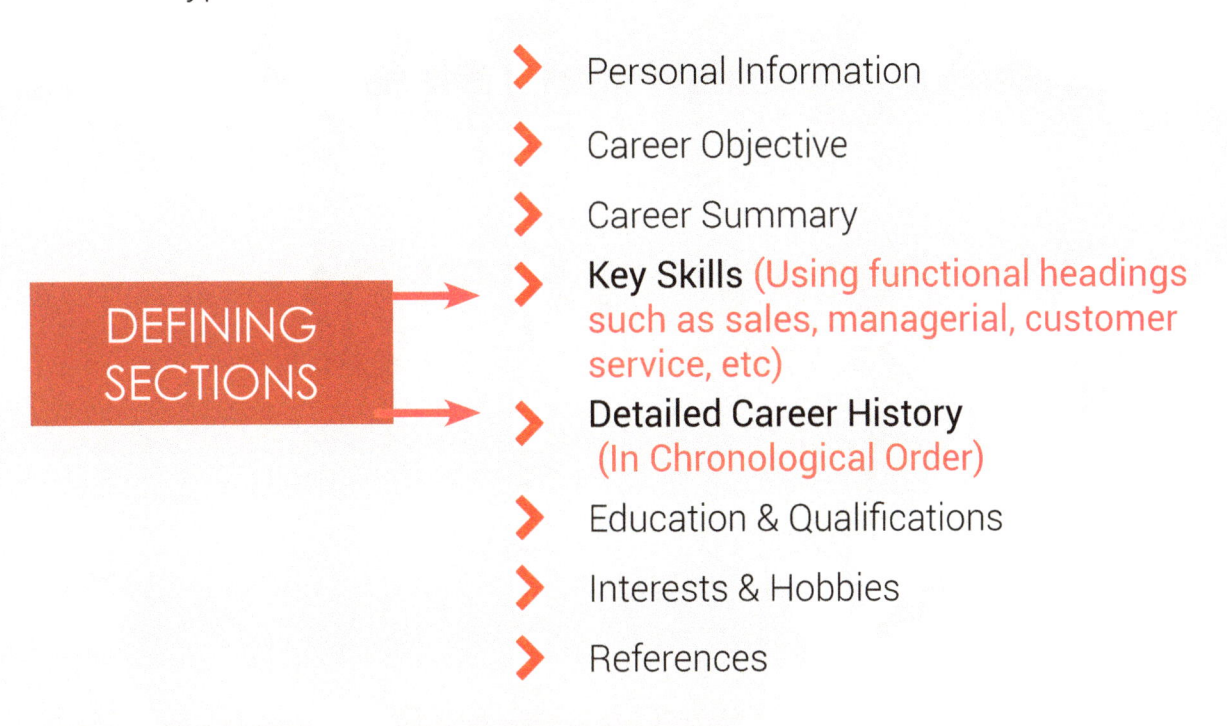

- Personal Information
- Career Objective
- Career Summary
- **Key Skills** (Using functional headings such as sales, managerial, customer service, etc)
- **Detailed Career History** (In Chronological Order)
- Education & Qualifications
- Interests & Hobbies
- References

DEFINING SECTIONS → Key Skills, Detailed Career History

> With this format, you will include both the key skills and a detailed career history. Key skills will come first, with experience directly following.

OUTLINE

MODIFIED COMBINATION

For the purpose of a cabin crew position, I will take you through a slightly modified version of the combination format. This format has shown to be the most effective and rounded approach.

You may, of course, modify this if another format is better suited to you. Simply use the guidelines provided for that format.

For the purpose of the cabin crew position, I have listed below my recommended résumé sections, in their suggested order:

1. Personal Information
2. Objective Statement
3. Key Skills
4. Employment History
5. Education & Qualifications
6. Certifications
7. Activities & Interests
8. References

PERSONAL INFORMATION

A rather obvious section, so I'll keep it brief.

At the beginning of the résumé you are going to want to include your name, your home mailing address, your telephone number(s), and your e-mail address. If you have both temporary and permanent addresses, you may include them both.

OBJECTIVE STATEMENT

My objective.... To get the job duh!!!

Yes, that may well be true, but the objective statement requires more than "Hire me, I want the job"

Instead, the objective should define your career goals while also positioning you as the ideal candidate for the position. It is a brief and targeted statement that gives your résumé focus and a great opportunity to show how your skills relate to the airline and the position.

QUICK TIP

If you are going through a career change or are currently working freelance, the objective statement is especially useful as it demonstrates that you have given your career direction due consideration, while also explaining any inconsistencies that may exist.

COMMON MISTAKES TO AVOID

MISTAKE #1

Making it all about you

> I have always loved to travel and am looking to join a prestigious airline that has lots of amazing destinations and where I can get cheap flights while meeting handsome wealthy men in first class.....

Okay, I am laying that one on thick, but you see my point. The objective is not about you or your needs, it is about what you bring to the airline.

MISTAKE #2

Being vague

> Looking for a job as cabin crew with an airline where I can apply my extensive skills and experience.

Hmm, that's not very enticing is it?

Would you want to go through the time and expense of bringing this person to interview when they have some undefined skills and experience, and who seems to not care which airline they work for?

No, and neither does the airline.

MISTAKE #3

Offering no value

> I have extensive skills in marketing and development...

STOP!!! Back up a bit.

How is this relevant to a cabin crew position? That's right, it isn't. Next...

If you do come from a background that seems unrelatable, such as marketing and development, dig deeper. Instead of marketing, the ability to influence could be used, and, instead of development, the ability to manage a team.

Now those would be kick ass skills to include.

MISTAKE #4

ZZZZZZZ

> My name is Jane Doe and I come from London, England. I have been working in finance, but I want to make a move to working as cabin crew. I have lots of skills, such as teamworking, customer service, and leadership. I also worked within......... and on, on on, and on......

Just remember that this is a brief statement, not an essay. zzzzz sorry, dozed off there for a second. What were we talking about?

You get my point. Keep it short and snappy.

HOW TO WRITE A SIZZLING OBJECTIVE

When writing your objective statement, there are four key points to keep in mind that will make it smoking hot.

- **Be specific**
- **Focus on the benefits you offer**
- **Keep it short**
- **Make it relevant to the position**

USE AIRLINE KEYWORDS

Here is where the research you conducted in the first module will begin to pay off.

To make your objective even more powerful and specific, you are going to insert the airline's own **person specification keywords** right into your objective. This is highly targeted and makes it easier to select qualities that the airline considers most valuable.

EXAMPLES

A **hard working** and **reliable** customer service advisor looking to apply 3+ years of **customer facing** experience and excellent **interpersonal skills** to a **cabin crew** role within Fly High Airlines.

Seeking a **cabin crew** position with **Fly High Airlines** where my **customer relations** experience and warm **interpersonal** style can be effectively used to provide passengers with a **first class** and **welcoming** experience.

Friendly and **enthusiastic** nurse looking to bring excellent **interpersonal** and **communication** skills, and 4+ years of experience within the **health care** industry to the role of **cabin crew** within **Fly High Airlines**.

A **professional** and **reliable** travel operator with 5+ years of experience within a **customer facing** and **teamwork** oriented role looking to bring an **enthusiastic** and **personable** nature to the role of **cabin crew** with **Fly High Airlines**.

ACTION STEP

Write your objective statement
Using the examples above, and the key skills you developed in module one, have a go at writing out your own statement.

MY OBJECTIVES

Prominent key skills to include:

Key skills are covered in detail on the next section, so you may refer to that

My best personal qualities:

Objective statement
Sample 1

Objective statement
Sample 2

KEY SKILLS

Ah ha. My favourite bit.

The key skills section provides a fantastic opportunity for you to quickly express your suitability for the role and show what transferable skills you will bring. It will also bulk out your résumé with the keywords that will be picked up by OCR scanning technology (More on this later).

Key skills can be those gained through your work experience or hobbies, even thorugh your studies and voluntary placements. This is why they are so valuable, especially if you have a short career history.

THREE CATEGORIES

Key skills fit into the following three distinct categories:

- **Transferable Skills**
- **Aptitude Skills**
- **Job Related Skills**

TRANSFERRABLE SKILLS

Transferable skills are generally **learned skills** and include those that can be picked up from your hobbies and personal interests, volunteer work, employment or education and can be transfered across to any industry or position. The transferable skills airlines are interested in include:

- Teamwork
- Foreign Languages
- Time Management
- Decision Making
- Customer Service
- Problem Solving
- Leadership & Management

APTITUDE SKILLS

Aptitude skills tend to overlap transferable skills, however, aptitude skils are those that are **inherited** as part of your character. Aptitude skills could include:

- Initiative
- Positive Nature
- Interpersonal Skills
- Tenacity
- Communication
- Loyalty
- Adaptability
- Friendly / Sociable
- Motivation
- Logical

JOB RELATED SKILLS

Job related skills are those that are specific to an industry. The key here is to find relatable skills within that industry that could become transferable. For instance:

Profession	Transferable Skill
Hairdresser	Customer Service
Tour Guide	Public Speaking
Nurse	First Aid & empathy
Travel Agent	Currency Conversion
Call Centre Op	Handling Complaints
Interior Designer	Managing People
Self Employed	Self Starter
Technical Support	Explain complex information clearly

Whatever jobs you have held, look for a transferrable and relatable skill.. Hightlight those as much as possible. Suddenly a seemingly irrelevant position can be seen as highly valuable.

EXAMPLE STATEMENTS

Once you have picked out 4 or 5 key skills, elaborate with **short** statements that provide insight to how you have **applied** these in the past. Here are some examples:

Extensive Interpersonal Skills
Working as a personal trainer for the past 5 years has given me first hand experience working very closely with people from all backgrounds and of all ages.

Team Spirited and ability to use my own initiative
Working as a waitress has given me an opportunity to develop my team working skills to a high standard, but it has also taught me to use my own initiative when working under pressure.

Problem Solver
Working as a freelance designer has given me an opportunity to develop finely tuned problem solving skills. I am able to think fast on my feet and deal effectively with challanges that create a positive outcome.

Strong customer service skills
As part of my job being a call centre handler, I have had the opportunity to develop a very rounded skill set that enables me to be empathetic to the customer, while also having the company interests in mind in order to ensure the best possible outcome for all concerned.

MY KEY SKILLS

Transferable skills

Aptitude skills

Job related skills

EMPLOYMENT HISTORY

Employment history should be displayed starting with your most recent position, working backwards and include the following elements:

- Name of employer
- Position held
- Period of employment
- Duties performed
- Achievements

DESCRIBING DUTIES

When describing your duties, there are three key points to bear n mind, these are:

- Use Short Action Phrases
- Make It Relatable
- Focus On Results

ACTION PHRASES

Action phrases offer greater impact than compete sentences or generic job descriptions because being short and punchy allows for easy scanning. Here are some examples of such phrases:

- Supervised and trained a team of four junior-level stylists
- Manage and maintain a customer base of over 100 clients
- Maintain up to date records of customer accounts
- Ensure customer comfort and satisfaction
- Assist with enquiries and resolve complaints

RELATABLE

As we discussed earlier, the points of the job you want to extract and highlight, are those that are relatable to the position of cabin crew.

Notice how breaking down the job of an interior designer below can appear totally different, depending on the words we use. Same job, different outcome and impression.

AVOID THIS

- Develop & design interior concepts
- Consider materials and analyse costs
- Source products
- Survey building
- Blah, blah, blah...

DO THIS

- Discuss **client** requirements
- **Communicate** & negotiate with suppliers
- **Collaborate** with a **team** of designers, architects and suppliers
- **Supervise** contractors to ensure the **customer** requirements are met

While the first example has no relevant keywords, the second has plenty. Which resume do you think will fair better in the recruitment process?

RESULTS/ACCOMPLISHMENTS

If you have any notable achievements that can be quantified, be sure to mention those too. Here are some notable achievements worth mentioning:

- Increased customer loyalty or satisfaction
- Decreased customer complaints
- Developed an idea that saved time or money, increased productivity, etc.
- Awards won
- Promotions earned

Even those little compliments your supervisor or managers have made informally can add weight to your application and make for a good story to tell during your interview, so try to remember anything that may be relevant.

Did you make a suggestion for improvements that your superior was particularly impressed by? Did you have an idea for a new service that was implemented? All these things matter.

MINIMISE FRAGMENTATION

If you have a fragmented work history, it will give the impression of a job hopper and this is something you will want to avoid.

The good news is there are many things you can do to draw attention away and minimise the impact . So let's take a look at the options.

COMBINE JOBS

Where several similar consecutive jobs appear or were provided by the same agency, you can combine them into one chunk, for example:

> **2004–2006 // Front Desk Clerk**
> Aztec Hotel & Spa, Bloomfields Leisure, Trina's Hair & Beauty Salon

> **2001–2003 Customer service manager**
> CS Employment Agency

For summer jobs, you can avoid listing listing specific dates by using a range, for example:

Summer 20xx to Spring 20xx.

ELIMINATE POSITIONS

There are times when it is beneficial to simply drop a position from your résumé. Take a look at the chart below to determine if this could be right for you.

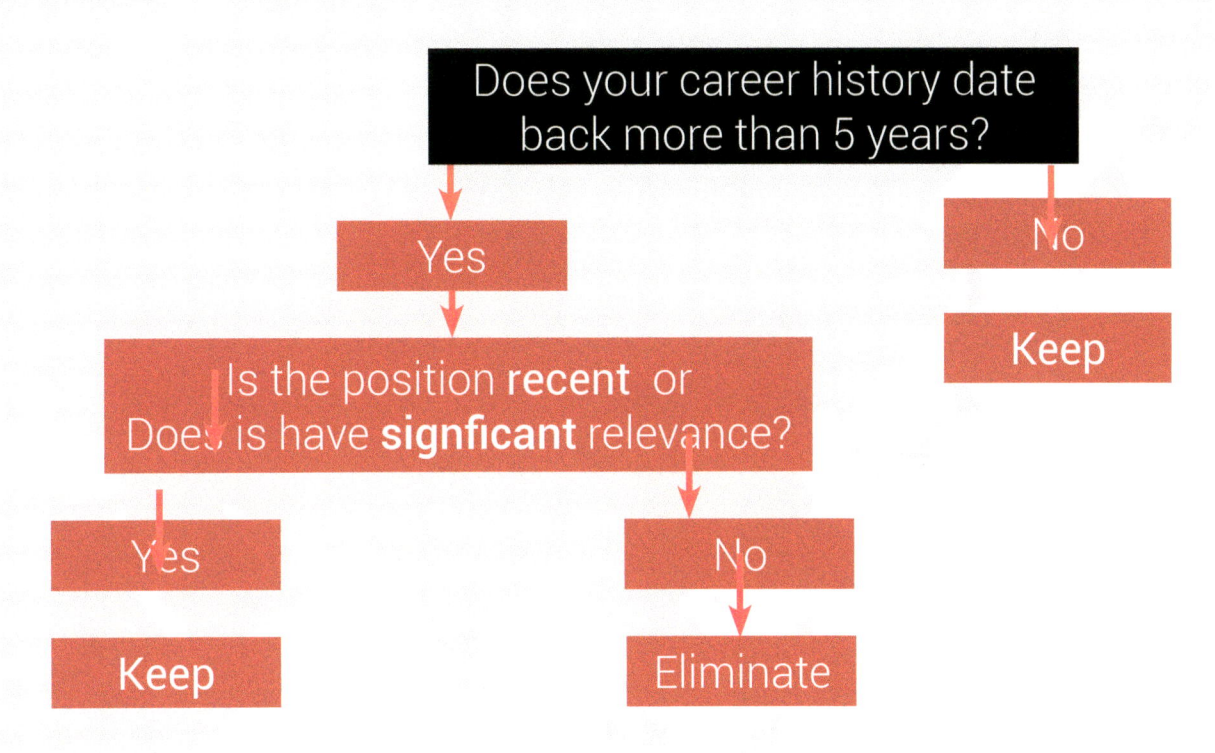

Does your career history date back more than 5 years?

- **No** → Keep
- **Yes** → Is the position **recent** or Does is have **signficant** relevance?
  - **Yes** → Keep
  - **No** → Eliminate

FILL THE GAPS

If you have gaps in your career progression, but were doing something notable during that time, paid or unpaid, you could insert this into the gap to eliminate any unceccesary questions or concern. For instance:

> **2004–2006 // Fitness Instructor**
> Bloomfields Leisure

> **2006-2007 // Traveled around Europe   or   Study Break**

> **2007–2012 // Personal Trainer**
> Wilson Gym

When filling the gaps, observe caution about revealing too much about your personal circumstances. Revealing that you had taken maternity leave will highlight your parental status. Although this may seem harmless, it's not something to advertise when seeking employment.

QUICK TIP

Employment history is a broad term that can include relevant internships, summer or seasonal jobs, part time work, and voluntary placements. Even helping your pops with his self employment business or babysitting can be included if you are struggling to provide relevant experience.

If you have major gaps to fill, take a look at what you were doing during those gaps and see if you can transfer and relate that across.

ACTION STEP

Write out your employment history. Remember to include action phrases and key skills

EMPLOYER:

Position held:

Period of employment:

Duty statements:

Achievements:

EMPLOYER:

Position held:

Period of employment:

Duty statements:

Achievements:

EMPLOYER:

Position held:

Period of employment:

Duty statements:

Achievements:

EDUCATION & QUALIFICATIONS

This is a simple one.

Starting with the most recent and working backwards, include the schools/colleges/universities you have attended. Within each entry, include the year of completion ("In progress" or "expected" are acceptable) and award(s) you achieved.

Easy peasy.

If you are a mature candidate, and your qualifications go bad a way, you may leave off your high school and any dated qualifications that are irrelevant. These will only draw unneccesary attention to your age.

MY QUALIFICATIONS

Establishment:

Year of completion:

Award recieved:

Establishment:

Year of completion:

Award recieved:

Establishment:

Year of completion:

Award recieved:

CERTIFICATIONS

If you have attended any formal certification courses that are relevant, be sure to include these. Examples could be:

- FIRST AID
- LIFE SAVING
- FOOD HYGIENE
- TEACHING

LANGUAGES

If you have more than one language ability, indicate whether you speak, read, and/or write the language, and include the level to which you are proficient, such as: native, fluent, proficient or basic conversational ability.

If you only had High School training that you only remember two words from, you may want to leave that aside.

MY CERTIFICATIONS

Awarding company:

Year of completion:

Award recieved:

Awarding company:

Year of completion:

Award recieved:

Awarding company:

Year of completion:

Award recieved:

MY LANGUAGE SKILLS

Language spoken:

Fluency:

Proficiency:

Language spoken:

Fluency:

Proficiency:

Language spoken:

Fluency:

Proficiency:

ACTIVITIES & INTERESTS

Recreational interests reveal a great deal about your personality and create depth to your character. Better yet, they also serve as excellent sources of additional skills and experiences which can be advantageous if you lack certain skills and/or experience.

Most candidates miss this vital opportunity and fill the section with meaningless list statements or unprofessional revelations. Take a look at the following examples, and you'll understand the difference some fine tuning can make.

AVOID THIS

Reading, watching television, going to the movies, socialising, traveling.

AND DEFINITELY AVOID THIS

I enjoy spending time with my mates, hitting the town and going out on the razz.

DO THIS

I have been a keen netball player for as long as I can remember and am an active member of Anytown women's netball club where I have been captain of the team for 3 years.

I have an active interest in nature, and regularly get involved with and manage conservation assignments.

To relax, I attend yoga and meditation classes, which help to keep me focused and relieve any buildup of stress.

> The statement on the right gives an immediate impression of someone who is balanced and committed. The interests highlight several admirable qualities such as team spirit and leadership, and it also details methods of stress management. A recruitment officer would form a positive impression based on a statement such as this.

MY INTERESTS & ACTIVITIES

Interest or activity

Transferrable skills:

Statement:

MY INTERESTS & ACTIVITIES

Interest or activity

Transferrable skills:

Statement:

MY INTERESTS & ACTIVITIES

Interest or activity

Transferrable skills:

Statement:

REFERENCES

The inclusion of reference information is completely optional. When listing your references, be sure to include:

Company
Contact Name
Job Title and Date of Employment
Telephone Number & Email
Mailing Address

If you decide not to include details, simply state "References are available on request"

Always gain permission from those you state as your referee. You don't want a referee to refuse to provide a reference as this will reflect negatively.

MY REFEREES

Company:

Contact name:

Job title:

Date of employment

Telephone number

Email address

Mailing address

MY REFEREES

Company:

Contact name:

Job title:

Date of employment

Telephone number

Email address

Mailing address

OPTIMISE

APPEARANCE

Have you ever noticed how dull and boring resume's look?

Well, you'll be pleased to hear that won't be yours. Now that you've compiled your data, it's time to optimise it's appearance so that it gains attention and actually gets read. For this, we will look at the following elements:

Colour   Length   Style

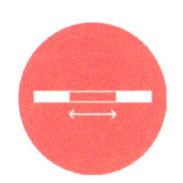

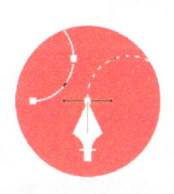

COLOUR

When used sparingly and consistently, colour can add life and interest to any dull resume. It can draw the eye to make the resume easier and more pleasant to read.

So, what exactly is consistent and sparingly?

COLOURED HEADINGS
with black text

HEADINGS WITH COLOURED UNDERLINES

❯ BLACK TEXT WITH COLOUR BULLET POINTS

HEADING WITH COLOURED BACKGROUNDS

LENGTH

For a cabin crew position, one or two pages is ideal. However, don't be constrained by this advice if doing so will mean that you have to squeeze your data in with a teeny tiny 8 point font.

If you do find your résumé going beyond this quota, just be sure that it isn't being fillied with unnecessary, unfocused or excessive detail.

If your career history dates back 10 or more years, you may choose to eliminate some of the older positions.

Note: Stick to single sided prints for a cleaner look.

STYLE

> **Paper**
> A quality, medium weight paper will give your resume an important feel and will show you have given it's presentation a conscious effort.

> **Margins**
> Whtie space on the page will keep your resume from looking cramped and overwhelming. Keep a margin of at least 0.75"

PERSONAL LOGO

If you want to add a creative edge, a personal logo is a great way to add a bit of sparkle that looks professional and stands out, but without additional clutter.

The logo need not be fancy or use special software, the autographed designs below were created with a font called Biloxi Script that can be downloaded for free from DaFont. The Jane Doe design simply has a line added to the J. Nothing fancy, but can make a difference.

Some free font ideas

Bromello

Angelina

Always forever

Bella Donna

EM
ELLETTE MORGAN

Carrie Ellise

Sandra Burton

Jane Doe

Jane Doe

OBJECTIVE

Seeking to pursue a cabin crew position with an airline that rewards commitment and hard work, and offers opportunities to progress.

KEY SKILLS

Communication Skills
Exhibits exceptional written and verbal communication skills, and is adept at communicating effectively with people at all levels, and in a manner appropriate to the audience.

Interpersonal Ability
Unsurpassed interpersonal skills with a proven ability to quickly develop and maintain relationships with customers and colleagues.

Customer Focus
Experienced at providing a high quality service to customers at all levels, and skilled at effectively dealing with and resolving complaints.

Team Spirited
Skilled team player who adapts quickly to different team dynamics and excels at building trusting relationships with colleagues at all levels.

EMPLOYMENT HISTORY

Freelance Hairdresser　　　　　　　　　　　　　Feb '03 – Present
- Manage and maintain a customer base of over 100 clients
- Consult and advise customers
- Ensure customer satisfaction
- Provide a friendly and professional service
- Maintain up to date records and accounts

Trina's Hair Salon | Senior Stylist　　　　　　　Aug '00 – Feb '03
- Supervised and trained a team of four junior-level stylists
- Hired work experience students
- Consulted and advised customers
- Ensured customer comfort and satisfaction
- Provided a friendly and professional service

---

16 Any Road • Any Where
Any Town • AN8 9SE
United Kingdom

+44 (0)4587 875848
Jane.Doe@Anymail.com

OBJECTIVE

My confident and friendly nature will enable me to fit in and complement your existing team

EMPLOYMENT CONTINUED...

Trina's Hair Salon - Junior Stylist — April '98 – Aug '00
- Consulted and advised customers
- Ensured customer comfort and satisfaction
- Provided a friendly and professional service

Macey's Hair Salon - Receptionist — July '96 – April '98
- Delivered the highest level of customer service
- Ensured customer comfort
- Provided a friendly and professional service
- Assisted with enquiries and resolved complaints

EDUCATION

Any College (2001) — NVQ 3 - Hairdressing
Any College (1999) — NVQ 2 - Hairdressing
Any College (1998) — NVQ 1 - Hairdressing
Any High School (1996) — 11 GCSE's (grade A–D)

CERTIFICATIONS

British Red Cross — Basic First Aid – Sept '06

LANGUAGES

Fluent in spoken and written Spanish
Basic conversational ability in French

ACTIVITIES & INTERESTS

I have been keen on netball for as long as I can remember and am an active member of my local netball club where I have been captain of the team for 3 years. I have an active interest in nature, and regularly get involved with and manage conservation assignments. To relax, I attend yoga and meditation classes, which help to keep me focused and relieve any build-up of stress

16 Any Road • Any Where
Any Town • AN8 9SE
United Kingdom

+44 (0)4587 875848
Jane.Doe@Anymail.com

Ellette Morgan

"I am looking to provide a memorable passenger experience as a member of the Virgin Atlantic cabin crew team"

Key Skills

Exceptional People Skills
Over the years, I have worked hard to develop my interpersonal and people skills so that I am able to deliver a level of service that is far and beyond what clients expect. I pride myself on my ability to engage with others on a professional and personal level.

Self Starter and Detail Oriented
Over the years, I have had to develop a strong sense of initiative and drive in order to remain at the forefront of business. I am a self starter who is able to work unsupervised without external motivation, but am also able to work as part of a unified team in order to meet deadlines and exceed client expectations.

Ability to work under pressure
Working to deadlines and making informed decisions is an ongoing part of my everyday life. Over the years, I have learnt to work under such pressure, while maintaining a high standard of service. Often, my best work is produced when there is an element of pressure involved.

Strong work ethic
My work ethic is one of my greatest assets. I take great pride in providing a great service and exceeding expectations. I take great pride in going that extra mile.

Career History

Graphic and Web Designer — July 05 - Present

- Liasing with clients during the initial briefing and offering ongoing support
- Negotiating and liasing with a team of contractors and suppliers
- Project management and supervision of work on site
- Working out costs and preparing estimates
- Ensuring customer satisfaction and demonstrating empathy towards clients
- Resolving any problems or faults during the work process
- Business management activities, including bookkeeping and tax returns, marketing and public relations

Nail technician — December 01 - July 05

- Consult and advise clients
- Make clients feel comfortable and welcome
- Ensure client satisfaction
- Initiate hygiene procedures and safe usage and storage of chemicals
- Manage and maintain a customer base of over 100 clients
- Provide a friendly and professional service
- Maintain up to date records and accounts

Ellette Morgan

Continued from page 1.

Education Summary

National Design Academy (2015)
Foundation Degree in Interior Design (Distinction)

National Design Academy (2013)
AIM Level 3 Diploma in Interior Design

Filton College (1997)
BTEC First Diploma in Performing Arts

Patchway High School (1996)
7 GCSE's

Certifications

First Aid (2010)
St John's Ambulance

Advanced First Aid (2011)
St John's Ambulance

Health & Safety (2012)
City of Bristol College

Personal Interests

I like to keep myself fit and healthy, and so I maintain a very active lifestyle which includes regular trips to the gym and yoga classes. I also have an interest in the fitness and bodybuilding competition industry, and have recently began competing myself. I first took to the stage last year at the Miami Pro show where I placed 6th. Not only is this one of the greatest challenges of my life, it also demonstrates my greatest strengths which is my determination and dedication.

I love to run, and often run 5 miles to keep me focused and relieves any build-up of stress. Not long ago before the fitness show, I was involved in the Bristol 10k where I raised over £1000 for the 'Make-a-Wish Foundation'. This marathon was definitely a challenge.

I also have a love for the aviation industry, so I often take weekends away to the Renaissance hotel in Heathrow, where I book a room overlooking the runway. This is where I get my inspiration to write and design, and also set goals for the future. More recently, I have also begun taking flying lessons. One day I would love to achieve my Private Pilots Licence (PPL).

> "The flight is part of the travel experience and I would like to be involved in making it just as memorable as the destination."

OCR TECHNOLOGY

To facilitate more efficient processing of résumés, and applications, airlines use a computerised tracking system. This system uses OCR (Optical Character Recognition) technology.

This technology scans for specific keywords that indicate a particular set of skills, qualifications and experience.

Following the scan, a score will be awarded based on the number of 'hits'. From this score, the system will either generate a letter of invitation, or a letter of rejection.

To ensure a high score, and an invitation letter, it is essential that you learn and inject as many keywords as possible throughout your resume. Following are some sample power statements and power verbs to give you an idea what you can indlude.

- » Good communication and interpersonal skills
- » A confident and friendly personality
- » Extensive customer service experience
- » Confidence in dealing with a range of people
- » The ability to work effectively in a team
- » Ability to handle difficult customers firmly and politely
- » Ability to stay calm, composed and focused under pressure
- » The ability to be tactful and diplomatic, but also assertive

Action verbs express action. They are positive, powerful and directive, and should be used abundantly throughout your résumé. Here are just a few examples:

- Arranged
- Assisted
- Communicated
- Conveyed
- Directed
- Explained
- Expressed
- Generated
- Guided
- Handled
- Improved
- Incorporated
- Interacted
- Listened
- Participated
- Persuaded
- Provided
- Resolved
- Suggested
- Trained

ACTION STEP

Prepare your resume

Using the above guidelines, and the information you have compiled, have a go at creating your compelling resume.

YAY

And there you have it... A powerful and optimised resume that will be sure to get you noticed.

The final step before you submit, is to walk away. Put it to one side for the evening or a few days. When you come back with fresh eyes, you'll be able to make improvements and perform a final proofread.

When proofreading, read it aloud, check line by line, ask a friend to check it over and read it backwards. This will ensure the most accuracy.

PAGE 130

YOUR PHOTOGRAPHS

A VISUAL CUE

The requisition of photographs is so much more than a simple vanity requirement, and I cannot emphasise their importance enough.

Not only will they serve as a visual reminder for the recruiters to refer back to throughout the assessment process, but they are also used to make hiring decisions long after the interview is over.

Airlines place a great deal of value on the photographs, and some will even have very strict requirements about their presentation.

For this reason, it is important that you use the following guidelines to create the very best lasting impression.

MODULE OUTCOME

It would be practically impossible for me to delve into the photo requirements of each and every airline and, by the time you read this book, those requirements may even be outdated because the industry and recruitment practices change so fast.

So, within this section I'm going to break things down into the two aspects that are universal and timeless. These are:

OVERALL PRESENTATION

YOUR APPEARANCE

PRESENTATION

The style of photographs you submit all depends on the airline you are applying to join. Casual shots may be pefectly acceptable to an airline who promote a casual and fun service, but appear sloppy and inapporpriate to one which places high regard on being professional.

Casual shots do present a much higher risk of rejection and, as such, I always err on the side of caution and provide more formalised shots. But, fear not, an airline that has a high regard for the standard of photographs will always provide you with firm requirements for the submission of your very final photos.

These guidelines simply compliment those given or provide you with some answers where guidelines don't exist.

The outline I will provide you with are based on the strictest of standards and best practice I have come across. They are professional and are a perfect solution if you are to be taken seriously.

Having said that, if you are looking to apply to an airline such as Soutwest or Virgin, who have a fun and relaxed attitude, you may relax these guideliens slightly according to your own judgement. The only thing I will say is absolutely no bikini shots and definitely no party pieces. These are still recruitment photos, and smart casual should be the minimum standard.

DIY OR GO PRO?

Similar to the advice given opposite, this decision will be based on the what the airline requires and, again, this varies from airline to airline.

Unless otherwise stated, it's generally okay to submit DIY photos along with your application, provided they are of a good standard. It's only when the interviews are complete and formal submission of your application file is submitted for final review that additional requirements will be provided.

So, don't worry too much at the outset, just submit the best photos you can, according to the guidelines in this book and you'll be alerted if changes need to be made.

When it comes to your final photographs, the requirements may change. This is particularly true with Emirates who will only accept professional studio photos. In such cases, you must adhere to those guidelines precisely.

You can always ring the HR department if you really are unsure. That's what they are there for.

STRICT REQUIREMENTS

Each airline will have its own specific requirements and these will be advised when you apply. It is important that you follow the directions given exactly, as some airlines are very strict about presentation..

I am not kidding. There are some airlines who will not accept your application if the photos fall short of the requirements stated.

It's easy to get caught up in vanity, heck I fell into that trap myself as you'll learn on the following page, but these photographs are not for admission into America's Next Top Model. They are for security and recruitment purposes.

As long as you stick to the guidelines provided by the airline and those set out within this guide, you'll have the very best chance of success.

SETTING THE SCENE

A solid backdrop will produce a clean and uncluttered appearance. If possible, use a contrasting colour to avoid blending into the surroundings. White or pastel shades are great choices.

If you are going the DIY route, please don't be tempted to use bed sheets as these look sloppy. Instead, you can pick up a very inexpensive white backdrop on eBay and Amazon, or find a clean white wall

Emirates are very specific with the backdrop, so be sure to follow those exactly. Get in the studio and have your photos taken on a white backdrop without any props. No exception.

CASE STUDY

After my final interview with Emirates, I recieved a telephone call from the recruiter who interviewed me advising that the photographs I had submitted weren't up to their standard and would likely be rejected by their Dubai HR team. She gave me full instructions for the photograph requirements and asked that I resubmit them before my application was sent off for final processing and a hiring decision made.

I submitted a new set of photographs according to the specifications, and I was again told they would be rejected due to being digitally processed. At that time in my life, I was fearful of the camera and appearing unphotogenic so I done another set and attempted to process them so the recruiter wouldn't know they were digital. It didn't work, she called me once again to request a correction.

By this time, I knew I had to get the photos right, and I did submit a set of photos that were accepted. This story demonstrates just how important photos can be, but also how a recruiter who believes in you can go out of their way to help you succeed, even after you fluff up a few times.

If you are applying with Emirates, please follow their standards exactly. No cutting corners.

QUICK TIP

Navigate over to Google Images or the airline website and take a look at how the cabin crew present themselves. How is their hair styled? Do they have a certain style of makeup applied?

Take some of the defining characteristics, and implement them for a subtle psychological boost that will have the recruiters seeing you as crew potential.

SIMPLE & ELEGANT

Most airlines prefer a very natural and fresh look, with clear skin, subtle eye makeup and a pop of **red** lipstick. It is a look that works well with all skin tones and is the epitomy of elegance. Try it for yourself.

The Huffington Post. (2017). Emirates Airlines Flight Attendants Reveal Just How Much Goes Into Their In-Flight Look. [online] Available at: http://www.huffingtonpost.com/2014/10/21/emirates-flight-attendants_n_5999818.html [Accessed 1 May 2017].

TRY IT YOURSELF

If you are not familiar with makeup application, why not book yourself in for a makeover. Take a cabin crew photo with you and ask them to replicate the look.

Or, if you'd like to give it a go yourself, take a look through some YouTube tutorials and give it a try. You can always wash it off if it doesn't turn out right.

GENTS GUIDELINES

Hair
Ensure your hair is well groomed. Facial hair will depend on the airline, but cleanly shaven is a safe bet, the decision is yours. If you do have facial hair, have it trimmed so it looks tidy. Go careful to avoid razor cuts.

Cosmetics
Yes, even for you. Don't worry, nobody will know. You simply want to dab a spot of concealer to cover any blemishes or under eye circles. Trust me, those of you willing to do this will look fresher. I won't tell if you don't.

Profile
Face and body facing direct to camera. Be sure feet are together, legs straight and both hands visible at your side.

Expression
A natural and welcoming smile

Scene
Clutter free and natural white background. This is especially important with Emirates. Emirates won't accept photos that have been digitally whitened, so don't skimp or try to cut corners.

Attire
Business attire is the way to go. This includes a jacket and a tie. You don't have to wear a blazer, but it's very cabin crew-esque. Think, Virgin Atlantic.

Pay attention to the details
Clean and tidy shoes and a pressed suit will add those finishing touches that will get noticed.

LADIES GUIDELINES

Hair
Hair is neatly groomed, with no flyaways or loose ends covering the face. I had photos rejected simply because I had a strand on hair coming down the side of my face.

Cosmetics
Makeup is subtle and natural, only using enough to enhance features and diminish blemishes, and a pop of colour on the lips for cabin crew appeal.

Profile
Face and body are facing direct to camera, with only a slight angle to the face. Be sure feet are together, legs straight and both hands visible at your side.

Expression
A natural and welcoming smile creates a friendly and inviting look.

Scene
Clutter free and natural white background. This is especially important with Emirates. Emirates won't accept photos that have been digitally whitened, so don't skimp or try to cut corners.

Attire
A business like fitted suit with jacket will ensure a professional appearance. Ladies, wear a skirt and nude tights.

Pay attention to the details
Clean and tidy shoes, manicured nails and a pressed suit will add those finishing touches that will get noticed.

These are the exact photos I submitted to Emirates that landed me the job in 2005.

ACTION STEP

Using the guidelines provided in the previous steps and the examples on the following pages, it's time to think about having your own photos done.

If you chose the DIY route, just follow the guidelines as closely as possible and try to have them taken with a decent camera.

And remember, from the neck down you're just the same as the next candidate, so make your smile bright and inviting.

YOUR APPLICATION FORM

... AND YOU'RE READY

Okay, so you have your resume and your photos, now it's time to begin the all important step of fillng in the application form.

Unlike a resume, which can be manipulated to a certain degree, an application form is far more rigid.

With its standardised format, comparisons between candidates and against the hiring criteria can be made momentarily, leaving no room for error.

Within this section of the module, I'll break down each area of an airline application form, giving you the best chance for success.

Access an airline application form

This step is optional, however if you have an airline in your sights, using their application form as you progress through this section will offer the most value to you.

You'll likely have to sign up for an online account, but don't worry, the airline won't see what you've input as long as you don't submit the form.

WELCOME

The great news is, by creating your resume first, you've already done most of the work. The majority of the information you have compiled will simply transfer over to your application form. Now isn't that great!

If you haven't completed the resume action steps, please go back and do those before progressing onto this section as I'll not repeat anything that has already been covered.

Within this section, I'll fill you in on the little nuances that are unique to the application form, these are:

DEALING WITH DISMISSALS

... ADDITIONAL INFORMATION ???

SUPPLEMENTARY QUESTIONS

HANDLING DISMISSALS

If you have a termination on your record, the airline will not care if the termination was unjust, unfair or has a good explanation, a termination is a big red flag and your applicatino will likely be rejected. Because of this, you'll want to do all you can to downlplay this.

There are several options you have for this, these are:

> **ELIMINATE THE POSITION**

> **ADJUST THE REASON**

> **EXPLAIN AND DOWNPLAY**

How you deal with this is completely your choice. I will advise you on each of these outcomes,. but you will need to make the final judgement call as to how to proceed.

ELIMINATE

In the first instance, you may choose to omit the information and the postiion from your application. Omitting details is not the same as telling an outright lie or making a false statement. You will simply be striking the position from the record.

Eliminating a position will only work if you can answer yes to one or more of the following questions:

» You have sufficient work experience beyond this position
» The position you were terminated from was a long time ago
» The position was temporary or very short term

The only thing I will say with regard to this particular strategy is, airlines operate in a very security conscious industry. You only want to take this route if necessary. Don't use it for any recent, long term or important roles as it is likely you will be found out evenutally.

ADJUST

A better option for a lot of people is to adjust the reason for dismissal. There are two options for this:

If you have just been fired from your most recent employment, the airline will not know unless you tell them. So you could mark your employment to present and leave it at that. If asked if they can call your employer for a reference, it would not raise any eyebrows if you respectfully decline due to your ongoing employment.

The second option is to take proactive measures to have the termination designation changed. If the termination occurred some time ago, it is more likely that the employer will be open to changing the designation if you accept responsibility and demonstrate a sincere regret for the situation.

Simply advise them that the termination is damaging your chances of gaining employment and you would like the designation changed to something neutral, such as laid off or resigned.

DOWNPLAY

If you would feel uncomfortable or unethical to omit such a detail and would prefer to take accountability for what happened, be sure to downplay the termination on your application form by simply stating 'will explain at interview'.

You will have some damage control to contend with, so remember to accept the mistake, don't blame others and don't make any excuses.

Stick to the facts, point out what went wrong and what you have learned from the experience.

Whichever route you take, there is a risk. Either you will not be hired by admitting to the termination or you may not be hired because you did not disclose it and were caught out. The decision has to be yours.

...ADDITIONAL INFORMATION

At the end of most application forms, you will be presented with some form of additional information box. This box may be ambiguous and simply state 'Additional Information', or it could be more specific, such as: Please state your reason for applying and why you feel you are suited to the position of cabin crew?

However this box is worded, this is an opportunity to sell yourself and should never ever be left blank. Use it to provide a power statement that summarises your experience, highlights your key skills, and shares your motives all within a few short paragraphs.

I would suggest a 3 part format for answering such spaces:

HIGHLIGHT WHAT YOU HAVE TO OFFER
EXPLAIN WHY YOU ARE SUITABLE
SUMMARISE YOUR STRENGTHS

Don't let modesty prevent you from mentioning your strengths, this is the opportunity to shine, however, keep this section to 2-3 short and punchy paragraphs and no more. You want to leave some cards on the table.

Remember to insert those power key words.

Consider the following example:

"As you will note, my application form highlights my extensive eight years experience within the retail industry. Within which, I have built a solid foundation of customer relations and team working experience, both of which have enabled me to sharpen my communication and interpersonal skills.

With the skills I have developed and the experiences I have dealt with as a customer relations manager, combined with my passion for the airline industry, my motivation to succeed and strong work ethic, I am confident that I will make a positive contribution to Fly High Airlines and excel as a member of the Fly High cabin crew team.

I would welcome the opportunity to meet with you to discuss this position and my background in more detail, and to explore ways I could contribute to the ongoing success of Fly High Airlines.

Thank you for your time and consideration. I look forward to hearing from you."

SUPPLEMENTARY QUESTIONS

In addition to the request for further information, the application may pose questions related to your motives for applying. These could include why you want to work for the airline, why you want to be cabin crew, or even why you believe you are the best person for the position.

Because the questions vary so much in nautre, and because I have provided detailed guidelines to formulating answers in module 4, I won't go into detail here. If you do find any questions beyond the scope of this section, please visit module 4 for further assistance.

Personal statement

POWER UP YOUR APPLICATION

If during this process you have noticed a lack of skills to put forward, all is not lost. There are several other steps you can take to power up your application and give it some pizazz. Take a look at the following options:

> **Boost your experience**
> Experience within a customer-facing role is vital, so if this aspect of your application is shallow or weak, you should certainly consider taking on some additional short-term volunteer or evening work to compensate and strengthen your candidacy. Taking on additional work will show initiative and demonstrate a willingness to work and improve.

> **Take on volunteer work**
> Volunteering is beneficial to your application in so many ways. Firstly, it will demonstrate a compassionate and caring side to your personality. Secondly, it will enable you to gain experience and flesh out your skill-set. And third, it will show that you are not motivated by monetary gain. As a side benefit, you will also gain additional referees who can vouch for you.

> **Learn new skills**
> Taking the time to learn new skills will demonstrate your continued dedication to self-improvement and your effort in readying yourself for the position. So consider signing up for mini courses that will be relevant to the position, such as first aid, languages, assertiveness, communication, and leadership. Neither will take much time or money, but the value added to your resume will be substantial.

> **Engage in extra-curricular activities**
> Extra-curricular activities can be a hidden gem when it comes to learning new skills and are often under-utilised. If you participate in team sports, it can demonstrate your ability to be a team player. If you coach little league, it will demonstrate your ability to be a leader and if you regularly participate in aerobic activities, it will show that you take pride in your health and fitness. So go out there and have some fun while boosting your candidacy all at the same time.

> **Mind the gap**
> If you are between work when you apply, this can create a damaging gap that will need some explaining or give the wrong impression about your motives. Rather than do nothing during this period of downtime, be proactive by taking on some volunteer work, learning a new skill or sign up for a short course at your local college..

What steps will you take to power up your portfolio?

Save or submit the form

Now that you have completed the application form, you may save it for future reference or sumbit it. The choice is yours. You have a very powerful application to work with and a whole host of positive information and facts to take forward with you into the next stage of the process. Well done.

Now it really is time to go bag yourself that job.

STEP THREE
PREPARE

Prepare to make an impression

PAGE 160

WELCOME

Now that you've researched the airline and compiled a kick-ass portfolio, it's time to get prepared for the interivew. So, in this step three, we'll explore how to dress to impress.

FIRST, THE MYTHS

Before we continue on I feel it is important to address some of the myths that are circulating with regards to appearance.

These myths usually imply that airlines only hire crew who embody perfect figures and harbour model looks. This is, quite frankly, utter nonsense. While there is no denying that airlines require candidates to be well groomed and portray a polished image, this element is usually taken out of context and to the extreme.

Appearance only matters in so far that you need to be within a healthy height to weight ratio, be well groomed and have no visible tattoos or piercings. It really is that simple.

And if the models in this book or on airlines websites concern you, those are just models whose job it is to look perfect,. Not to mention that they have been airbrushed to the max. It is simply marketing, and not reality.

Don't believe me? Think back to flights you have experienced or go check out the social media sites to see for yourself. Crew come in all shapes, sizes and appearances.

THE FIRST IMPRESSION

During the first few minutes of meeting you, the recruitment team will make judgements about your character and suitability based on your overall presentation and appearance. This means that your standard of dress, level of grooming and how you portray yourself through your body language and carriage are all being scrutinised. Therefore, if you are to succeed in creating that all-important positive first impression, it is essential that you make an extra effort to establish a presence.

There is no doubt that appearing professional is the key to creating the best impression at a cabin crew interview. The trouble is, being professional is only part of it. Put a robot into a suit and it too would look professional, but would the robot get the job? It is unlikely.

The fact is, airlines are not looking to hire a suit, but rather they are looking to hire an individual with a personality and character. So, dress smart and pay attention to your grooming standards, however, don't be afraid to inject your personality and sense of style into your outfit. The bottom line is, you need to feel good in what you're weearing.

Professional or not, if you are not feeling at your best it will show and you will not be maximising your opportunity.

LADIES STYLE GUIDE

STYLE

Presence is achieved when you look and feel good, so it is important to wear an outfit that you feel the most confident and powerful in. However, in order to stand out for the right reasons, it is important to achieve balance: Balance between how the outfit makes you feel and what impression it creates.

Your outfit should be thoughtful and demonstrate that you have made an effort. So buy the best quality garments that you can afford, and be sure they are clean and neatly pressed. The idea is to look business-like, yet stylish.

Tasteful, elegant and sophisticated are good objectives to aim for, and you'll want to avoid appearing flashy or overly sexy. Well-coordinated and tailored separates achieve this perfectly, as does a fitted dress in a conservative style: Conservative implying a modest neckline and appropriate length. A quality tailored jacket is a powerful piece that can tie a look together and create a streamlined and professional appearance.

Avoid heavy patterns, as these can appear overwhelming, and be sure to select wrinkle resistant fabrics, such as wool. Nothing looks more unprofessional or unprepared than rumpled clothes or wrinkled shirts.

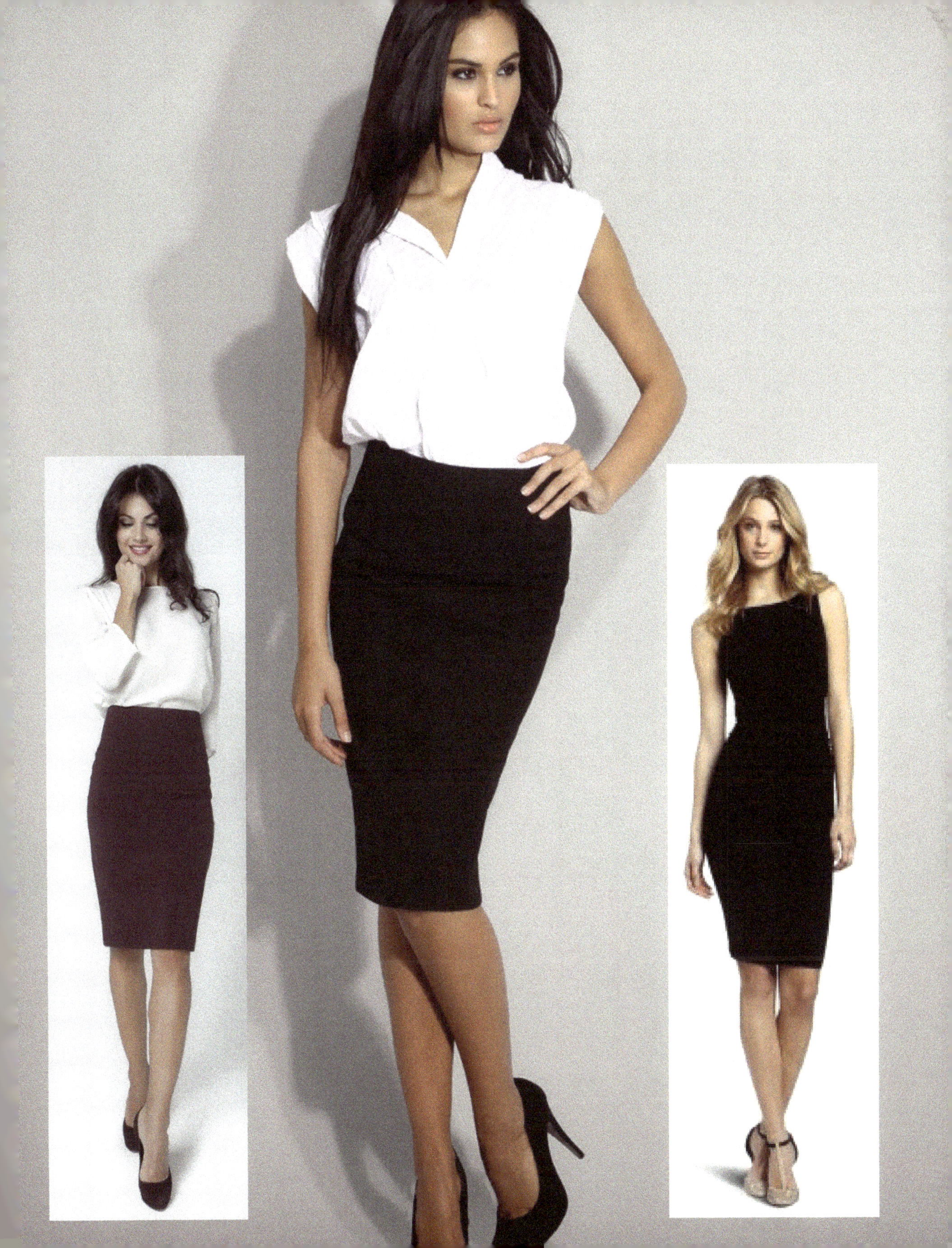

COLOUR

Colour is a powerful tool that can dramatically increase your chances of standing out. Used appropriately, colour will help you to convey confidence, express your personality and enhance your complexion. So, consider adding a splash of your favourite colour to your outfit for added pizazz.

How much colour you wear will depend on you. There is not necessarily anything wrong with wearing a red pencil dress provided you have the strength of character to pull it off and the colour is flattering against your complexion. However, such a bold statement piece should not be underestimated and must be worn with caution. If you choose to wear a bold piece, be sure that you have the courage of your convictions because you will certainly be noticed and expectations will be set much higher. You wouldn't want to be noticed for looking extremely uncomfortable or for looking washed out by an unflattering colour.

You don't need to be draped in colour to make an impact. In fact, the safest way to wear colour is to add subtle splashes through your accessories, accents or pop pieces. Subtle accents can bring out the sparkle in your eyes and liven up your outfit, without appearing overwhelming or degrading your professionalism.

Whatever you ultimately decide, a contrasting style will bring a sense of balance to the outfit. For a bold and striking colour, opt for a very conservative cut and for a pale tint, add life by selecting a striking style..

SHOES

The benefits of wearing heels are obvious. They make your legs look longer, shapelier and more feminine, so it is a good idea to wear them if you feel comfortable to do so. Killer heels may have the added butt lifting effect, however, this is not the look you want to achieve at an interview. Heels should be no higher than 3" and thin soles will appear more professional and elegant than thick platforms.

For those of you who are not used to wearing heels or are on the taller side, 1" inch heels will still provide the benefits of wearing heels without the excess height.

Only wear shoes which are clean and in good condition. Tatty shoes, with scuffed toes or heels will detract from the polished image you are trying to create. Open toes, sling backs and splashes of colour are perfectly acceptable as long as they are tasteful and not overly sexy or decorative fashion styles. Use your judgement.

HOSIERY

If wearing a dress or a skirt, pantyhose in plain nude or black are essential for creating a polished and professional image, as they will ensure your legs look perfectly smooth and blemish free. Be sure to select a good quality pair, as they will hug your curves better than cheaper alternatives and will be less likely to create the unsightly wrinkled effect around the knees and ankles. Be sure to spot check them before the interview to ensure that there are no runs or ladders and always have an emergency pair in your handbag for good measure.

GROOMING

For grooming, you can follow the same guidelines outlined in step two that you applied to your photographs. The same rules apply here.

A polished appearance, with clean and well groomed hair and attention to the details such as your nails and covering any blemishes is perfect. You needn't do more than this.

One extra note of caution if you are wearing perfume. Use a subtle scent suitable for daytime use. Overpowering scents can be off putting, less is more.

UNFAIR ADVANTAGE

Interviewers need to be able to visualise you in the position, so the very act of looking like you are already cabin crew will create a great psychological advantage.

Now, I am not implying that you find a suit in a matching colour to the airlines' uniform with hat and scarf to match. Sure this would make you stand out, but not for the right reasons. Subtlety is the key to success with this strategy. You're trying to capture the airlines aesthetic appeal, not look like you are attending a fancy dress parade.

The best way to pull this off is to look at the cabin crew who already work for the airline. Is red lipstick a part of the uniform? What are the typical hair grooming styles? Are their corporate colours muted, pale or bold? And what about the corporate culture? Is the airline energetic, carefree and fun loving, or conservative and professional? Understanding these aspects will help you to achieve the most appropriate interview look for each airline.

Injecting a splash of the corporate colour into your accessories is a great touch. Another is to tend to your grooming in the same way you would if offered the position. Understanding the corporate culture will further enable you to tailor your outfit according to the tastes of the airline. If the airline is famous for its fun and carefree corporate culture, you can be sure they will be more accepting of bold colours and unique styling, whereas an airline known for its conservative image may not be.

The effort you put in to this will show and it will be apparent that you have done your research to understand the airline's culture. The psychological impact this one trick can achieve is astonishing and should not be underestimated.

AVOID THESE FAUX PAS'

If you would like to be taken seriously, you need to avoid the following fatal mistakes.

1. Push up bra and plunging necklines
2. Bare midriff
3. Too much makeup or hair product
4. Unnecessary accessories
5. Wrinkled or unkempt clothes
6. Ill fitting garments
7. Cheap and translucent blouses
8. Scuffed or tatty shoes
9. Short skirt
10. Extremely high heels or large platforms
11. Bitten or over the top nails
12. Strong perfume

ACTION STEP

Pick out an outfit

Have a rummage around your wardrobe or visit your favourite clothing store for your perfect outfit.

GENTS STYLE GUIDE

When it comes to looking professional, the options for gents are no doubt limited. Formal business attire is essential for creating a professional, polished and streamlined look, however, when every other male candidate is also wearing business attire, how do you stand out from the crowd? It is the attention you pay to the finer details that will show that you have made an effort, and it is this that will get you noticed.

QUALITY & FIT

The key to looking your best in a suit is to pay special attention to fit and quality. A well-tailored suit, in a wrinkle free fabric, will create a polished and professional look that will surely set you apart from the rest. Off the rack suits are a popular choice because they are convenient and inexpensive, however, a ready to wear suit is often the worst option when making a good impression is your top priority. As such, it is advisable to purchase the best quality suit you can afford. A custom tailored suit is the obvious choice, however if finances will not stretch to this, purchase an off the rack suit and have some tailored alterations carried out for an inexpensive alternative.

Whichever option you choose, be sure to pay attention to selecting a good quality fabric. Natural fabrics are far better than synthetic fabrics or blends. In particular, wool, such as merino, cashmere and angora, will offer the best in comfort, wrinkle resistance, and longevity.

CONSIDER YOUR SHIRT

A good quality, 100% cotton shirt, with long sleeves is essential for appearing professional and crisp. White, ecru and blue are classic and conservative choices and should be your first choice.

Dark shirts are somewhat taboo as they are often considered a style choice, rather than a professional one. As such, you need to proceed with caution if this is what you feel most comfortable wearing. On the one hand it is important to wear what you feel confident and powerful in, but on the other, it is important to achieve balance: Balance between how the outfit makes you feel and what impression it creates. Airlines are no doubt much more open to personal style choices, however, it is a choice that may not be viewed favourably, no matter how powerful and confident it makes you feel. Therefore, it is far better to play it safe.

When it comes to choosing a collar, remember that it will frame your face. As such, you will want to select a collar that brings balance to your face shape. A wide spread collar will compliment a thin and long face well, while a classic point works better on a round face.

GROOMING

When it comes to grooming a good haircut and clean-shaven face are essential. A few days prior to the interview, have your hair freshly cut or trimmed and be sure to shave on the morning of the interview. Be careful not to cut yourself and try to prevent razor burn. If you do have facial hair, have it neatly trimmed.

Nails are another aspect that is often neglected and underestimated by male candidates. A manicure is an attention to detail that will be noticed and appreciated, so visit a manicurist a few days before the interview.

If you must wear cologne, be sure not to use too much as it can be distracting and suffocating.

CONSIDER YOUR TIE

The tie is an extremely important accessory, as it is often the first thing that a person notices.

Since it frames your face, it is important to consider the colour choice carefully because the wrong colour can suck the sparkle out of your complexion, leaving you looking dull and lifeless. When considering colour, assess how it interacts and enhances your complexion. Does red make your skin look bright, vibrant and well rested? or does it make you look sallow and washed out? Likewise, does blue bring a sparkle to your eyes, or does it make your complexion look muddy and ashen?

Pattern is another factor that needs consideration. Character ties and exotic patterns, while demonstrating personality, are not the ideal interview choice. Instead, opt for subtle stripes, simple designs or block colours for a classic and professional look.

For a strong and confident appeal opt for a larger knot, such as the Pratt or Windsor and aim for a length that falls to the same level as the belt buckle. Tie bars and clips may also be worn to keep the tie in place.

ACCESSORISE

Accessories are finishing touches and should be treated as such. This means that they should remain simple to complement your outfit. Cufflinks may be worn if you are wearing a buttonless shirt, and a leather belt with an understated buckle ought not be forgotten.

While a leather briefcase is unnecessary, a leather portfolio will look much more professional than carrying lots of loose papers.

When it comes to jewellery, the simpler and less of it, the better. One ring and a tasteful wristwatch is all that is necessary to project a professional image.

UNFAIR ADVANTAGE

Interviewers need to be able to visualise you in the position, so the very act of looking like you are already cabin crew will create a great psychological advantage. Now, I am not implying that you arrive in something too similar to the airlines' uniform; however, it doesn't hurt to capture an element of the industries aesthetic appeal.

The one item that captures this look the best is a fitted waistcoat. It is an element often under-utilised, but its stylish appeal works wonders within the airline industry.

Some of you may baulk at this idea, however, it is an element, which will set off your look. Not only do they create a business-like and streamlined appearance, but it will show that you have made an extra special effort. Take a look at the Virgin Atlantic uniform to get a sense of its style for yourself. If a waistcoat does fit in with your personal style, consider including it in your repertoire.

Don't want to look like a waiter? Heck, even top CEO's wear waistcoats, as does the famous footballer David Beckham. They are very suave. However, you should only wear one if you can do so comfortably.

AVOID THESE FAUX PAS'

If you would like to be taken seriously, you need to avoid the following fatal mistakes.

1. Short sleeves
2. Strong cologne
3. Too much hair product
4. Excessive jewellery
5. Wrinkled or unkempt clothes
6. Ill fitting garments
7. Scuffed or tatty shoes
8. Visible tattoos or piercings
9. Rubber sports watch
10. Bow tie or suspenders
11. Excessive facial hair

ACTION STEP

Pick out an outfit

Have a rummage around your wardrobe or visit your favourite clothing store for your perfect outfit.

IN CONCLUSION

While the advice and guidance given in this chapter may sound obvious, unnecessary and, even, unimportant, it has been my experience that many candidates fail to create an impression because they are either confused or uninformed about the standard of dress expected of them or because they neglect to pay enough attention to the details.

Following this guidance will not only multiply your chances of attracting the interviewers attention, but you will also stand out for having made an extra effort. Having said that, please use the information you gathered about the corporate culture to make you own judgement and adapt your attire as necessary.

In the grand scheme of things, it does not matter how well you are dressed or how much effort you have gone through if the rest of your delivery is poor. So, continue reading and you will discover important steps that will make you truly memorable.

STEP FOUR
ATTEND

It's time to bag the job

KEEP CALM

AND

ROCK YOUR INTERVIEW!

WELCOME

And you've made it to interview day.

You've done your research and are armed with juicy facts about the airline. You have your outfit prepared and are groomed to perfection.

This is it. It's time to go bag yourself that job.

Are you ready to get this done? Heck, I know you that you are. So let's do this...

MODULE OUTLINE

This module is split into two distinct sections, these are:

> **The Group Interview**

Here we will look at what you can expect, what the recruiters are actually assessing and looking for, and how to stand out for all the right reasons.

> **The Final Interview**

Within the final interview section, we'll delve into the questions you may be asked and I'll provide you with simple formulas so that you can formulate the most appropriate answer.

THE GROUP INTERVIEW

WHAT TO EXPECT

The assessment process varies considerably in length and structure depending on a number of factors. These factors include: The volume of applicants, whether the sessions are held within the airline's premises or a hotel establishment, and whether the sessions are open or invitation only.

Open days typically attract a high volume of candidates and, as such, will often be split over a series of days. Invitation only days, on the other hand, are kept much smaller in number and may span only a few short hours with final interviews conducted on the same day.

In either case, you will be asked to partake is a number of activities. These activities are designed to reveal your personality, competencies and potential for working as cabin crew and are likely to include a series of individual assessments, practical tasks, group discussions and role-play scenarios.

Arrival at the event can seem overwhelming, especially when faced with hundreds of applicants in attendance. You will likely be met with an atmosphere that is friendly and buzzing with adrenaline, but has an eerie sense of tension, as each candidate is anxious to get through the process. This atmosphere generally tapers off as the sessions get underway.

THE ICEBREAKER

The recruitment personnel will often start the day with a short introductory briefing and a breakdown of the intended days events. This session should last no more than 30 minutes or so, and allows for any remaining candidates to arrive before the event officially gets underway.

The icebreaker session may involve a short presentation about the airline followed by an open discussion session. During this time, candidates are encouraged to pose questions to the personnel about the airline and the position.

This session can be tricky because it's easy to stand out for all the wrong reasons.

If a question is asked that has already been answered within the airline literature, this will highlight a lack of prior research. A question that requires a lengthy answer will either annoy the recruiters or they will decline to answer, and that's never a good thing.

You'll also find that many of the more confident candidates make the mistake of getting carried away with their line of questioning in an attempt to stand out. Unfortunately, asking too many questions at this stage will only demonstrate a general lack of respect for others, who also have questions, and is also more likely to be misconstrued as arrogant, rather than confident.

If there's one tip I can give you, it's to bear in mind that this is only an icebreaker session. The recruitment personnel don't want to be answering a long list of questions and neither do they want to be giving long answers to complicated questions, so if you do want to ask a question, ask only ONE question, keep it brief and simple to answer.

And remember, you don't need to ask a question if you don't have one suitable. There will be plenty of opportunities to stand out as the day goes on. It's better to remain silent here than risk asking the wrong question.

So, what question should you ask? There are three types of questions that work well within this scenario, these are:

> Questions that demonstrate your research about the airline and the position
> Questions that highlight your enthusiasm
> Questions that reflect some depth to your motives

But honestly, each of these types of questions have the potential to require long-winded responses or may put the recruiter too much into the spotlight to perform. During this stage, I'd only ask a question if it is expected of you or you have a burning question that hasn't been answered through any prior means.

SELF INTRODUCTION

A lot of airlines will typically move into an introduction stage following the icebreaker session. And this my friend, this is where you can truly shine.

As well as learning more about you and your background, these self-introductions are an opportunity for the recruiters to assess how well you cope when addressing a group of people and how articulately you are able to communicate your message while under pressure. In their assessment, they will be looking for good delivery and a certain amount of charisma.

To deliver a self-introduction that makes an impact, here are some guidelines for you to consider.

Make it relevant
Use this opportunity to highlight your suitability for the job of cabin crew by sharing interesting facts about your present or most recent job, and your motives for making a career change.

Be spontaneous
A self-presentation which is spontaneous, rather than rehearsed, will add life and sincerity to your speech. Sure you can prepare a rough draft and familiarise yourself with it, but don't try to learn it by heart, as there is a risk of appearing forced, dull and robotic.

Inject personality
Show your passion and enthusiasm by injecting some emotion and personality into your presentation.

Be concise
Unless advised otherwise, keep it relatively short and focused. Thirty to Sixty seconds should be sufficient.

Rotate your focus
To give the impression of confidence and engage your audience, rotate your gaze and make eye contact with various members for three to five seconds each, then be sure to redirect your focus back to the recruiters to finish your presentation.

Beware of how you sound
Varying your tone, pitch, volume and pace will eliminate the risk of appearing monotone and make it enjoyable for others to listen to. If you are nervous, you may be more inclined to rush. It will help if you make a deliberate attempt to slow your pace slightly.

Consider this example
" Hi everyone. My name is Caitlyn and it's really nice to meet you all. I'm 27 years old and live in the bustling city of Bristol. I currently work as a personal trainer, which is a job I really enjoy, but I have always wanted to be cabin crew with ___ airlines because of it's fun corporate culture and innovative approaches to travel, which is why I am here today. I hope I can bring some pizazz of my own"

WHAT ARE THEY LOOKING FOR?

This is the one question I am asked, time and time again. So many candidates overanalyse the process, but the answer is actually very simple. So simple in fact that most of you you will already know what I am going to say.

The recruiters are assessing six key competencies. These are:

Communication skills	Interpersonal ability
Customer focus	Team spirit
Leadership	Initiative

And of course, your match with the corporate culture.

Because each airline will value these aspects differently, you'll need to be mindful of each, but also use your research to adjust your approach according to what you observe to be most valuable.

In order to determine these competencies, the assessors will be observing the following aspects:

- Your level of participation and interaction
- Your behaviour towards the activities and your peers
- Your communication and work style
- Your ability to think on your feet and react to external pressure
- Your ability to lead and willingness to follow

THE CONFUSION

Group tasks are designed so that assessors can view and assess these core competencies first hand, and how you behave during each task will be taken as a clear indication of how you may perform in reality.

While it goes without saying that how you behave during an interview is not going to be an accurate representation when compared with a real life scenario, it is through your involvement and behaviour, that assessors can identify positive and negative attributes first hand and be able to make better decisions.

Where most individuals often become confused is between the relevancy of the task and what is actually being observed.

Because some of the tasks bear no obvious relevance to the cabin crew role, it is easy to overlook the underlying motives and get caught up in the practicalities of the task instead. And herein lies the trick: **The outcome of the task itself is irrelevant.**

This is so important that it bears repeating. The outcome of the task itself is irrelevant. Let me explain this further....

Assessors are more concerned with how well you perform under pressure and in a team environment, how you communicate your ideas, how you interact with others and what role you assume than they are to see if you can decide your way out of being trapped on a desert island.

When you think back to the group tasks you have participated in, do you notice that they appear to have no right or wrong answer? That's because there is no right or wrong answer.

As an example, consider the following popular group topic:

Topic:

The plane has gone down over the Atlantic Ocean. There are eight survivors, but the one surviving life raft only has a capacity for four people. As a **team**, identify four survivors from the following list who you would save and state your reasons why. Select a spokesperson to **present** your decision and explain why you came up with the answer.

You (the flight attendant)	The pope
An ex army general	A surgeon
A pregnant lady	A child
An word class athlete	A nurse

Clearly there is no right answer to this topic, as you wouldn't want to decide such a fate for four people and the recruiters understand that such a decision would be difficult. So what is the point of this task?

Take another look at the topic and notice the words I have emphasised are 'team' and 'present'. These are the keys to this task.

Assessors are looking to observe how you interact as part of a **team**, and whether you demonstrate initiative and leadership by volunteering to **present** the information back to the rest of the group. Most candidates will focus on everything except for those two key points.

Let's take a look at another example: Singing.

Many candidates understand the concept of a discussion or role-play scenario, but just do not understand how singing bears any relevance. Again, this is very simple to comprehend if you read between the lines and understand the motives.

Task:

Many passengers ignore safety demonstrations because they feel they have heard it all before. In an effort to increase safety, Fly High Airlines is considering an overhaul of its safety procedures. As a **team**, come up with a new safety demonstration, which will encourage passengers to pay attention to these important briefings.

The demonstration can include appropriate humour, and must be sung according to the melody given to you on the back of the card. The outcome should be no more than **5 minutes** in length and **each individual** must play a role in the final presentation.

Within this task, you can see that team is once again emphasised, but the additional mention of a deadline and that each individual must participate tells us that your ability to follow the instructions and stick to the schedule is being observed, as is your own ability to take part.

Because the task focuses on singing, you can be sure the airline wants to see if you are willing to let go and have fun. This task is typical of airlines such as Virgin Atlantic and Southwest airlines who promote a service with a fun edge. You can be sure that the airline is sizing you up against its corporate culture during this task and, if you feel too modest to participate, you may want to reassess the corporate culture is a fit with your own style.

Even if you feel utterly silly and have the worst voice in the world, you should be standing confident as if you are Celine Dion or Christina Aguilera during this task because you can be sure that's what the receuiters want to see. In fact, having a bad voice can stand you in good stead during this task because you'll make people smile if you give it your best effort.

Make em smile and you'll bag that job.

TIPS FOR STANDING OUT

> **Have fun**
> However silly or irrelevant the tasks may seem, your active involvement is essential. So, rather than concern yourself about external details, just relax and allow yourself to enjoy the process. This positive viewpoint will reflect well on your character, demonstrate enthusiasm, and make the experience a fun filled one for you.

> **Contribute**
> Contributing ideas and making suggestions is another great way to demonstrate your enthusiasm and team spirit. It will show that you are able to express yourself and are keen to get involved.

> **Volunteer**
> There are times when no candidate wants to put their neck on the line, so volunteering is a great way to demonstrate your enthusiasm and it will show that you are not afraid to take the initiative.

> **Use names**
> Remembering people's names will demonstrate your ability to listen and pay attention to detail. Moreover, it will demonstrate a tremendous amount of respect for others and create a lasting impact.

> **Summarise**
> Summarising the main points of a discussion is a great way to move past awkward moments of silence and sticking points. The breathing room summarising creates will typically stimulate further ideas and encourage participation. Not only will your peers be grateful for the momentary relief, your communication and leadership ability will also be highlighted.

> **Be positive**
> When you choose to exhibit a positive spirit, people will naturally be drawn towards your character. So, be enthusiastic about the exercises you are asked to undertake and be encouraging towards others.

> **Be encouraging**
> If any members of your team remain reserved, encourage their involvement by asking if they have an idea, suggestion or opinion. This shows empathy, consideration and team spirit. This is such a great quality to demonstrate, and one that is often missed by over-zealous candidates.

> **Support the leader**
> If you have one or more powerful characters in your team who have stepped up to the leadership position, show your support in helping them to succeed within that role. Just because a team has a leader, doesn't mean everyone else should fall by the wayside. Showing support will show the ultimate team spirit.

...AND SOME TO AVOID

> **Over involvement**
> Getting involved and showing enthusiasm in a task is fantastic, but over involvement and incessant talking can leave others struggling to get involved and may transfer across to assessors as arrogance. Always provide others with an opportunity to provide their opinion.

> **Under involvement**
> For assessors to make an informed assessment, active involvement from each individual is essential. Those who are unable to get involved, for whatever reason, will surely be eliminated.

> **Entering into a dispute**
> Conflicting views are natural, however, a group assessment is neither the time or place to engage in a hostile dispute with other candidates.

> **Criticising**
> Even if your intentions are honourable and the feedback is constructive, criticising another candidates opinions, actions and ideas may be perceived as an attack. An assessment day is neither the time nor the place.

> **Being negative**
Making negative remarks or exhibiting frustration over tasks, peers or previous employers , no matter how harmless it may seem, will raise serious concerns about your attitude and ethics.

> **Being bossy**
There is nothing wrong with striving for excellence, however, being dominant and imposing your ideas on others is overbearing and intimidating. This always leads others to feel incompetent.

> **Not listening or talking over others**
Neglecting to listen to instructions leads to misinterpretations and displays a general lack of enthusiasm. Not listening or talking over others is ignorant and disrespectful.

GET INVOLVED...

I know it goes without saying, and I've covered this briefly above, but it bears repeating that it is only through your active involvement that recruiters are able to assess your suitability and identify your positive attributes. So however silly or irrelevant the tasks may seem, or how difficult it is to get your opinion across, your involvement is essential.

Rather than concern yourself about external details, just relax and allow yourself to enjoy the process. This positive viewpoint will reflect well on your character, demonstrate enthusiasm, and make the experience a fun filled one for you.

I understand that it can be difficult to get involved when you are in a group of individuals who have big personalities. They set off on a tangent, leaving you feeling like you are on the outside struggling to get in. While these conditions do pose a difficult challenge, it is absolutely essential that you do what you can to be included. Raise your hand if you need to, but whatever you do, don't remain on the outside.

If you suffer from nervousness, understand that it is okay to be nervous, even permissible, but allowing your nerves to keep you from getting involved is not. It is better to risk displaying your nerves than it is to remain silent. At least the recruiters will appreciate your effort.

…BUT DON'T OVERDO IT

Getting involved and showing enthusiasm in a task is fantastic, but over involvement and incessant talking can leave others struggling to get involved and may transfer across to assessors as arrogance.

If you do notice that other members of your team remain reserved or appear to be struggling to get involved, encourage their involvement by asking if they have an idea, suggestion or opinion. This is a clear indication of empathy, consideration and team spirit and it is these qualities that recruiters will be impressed by.

ROLE PLAY SCENARIOS

Role-play scenarios may be performed with other candidates as a pair or within a group.

The scenarios will bear some relation to the demands of the job and are likely to include:

Intoxicated passenger	Disorderly behaviour
Terrorist threat	Disruptive child
Toilet smoker	Abusive behaviour
Fearful passenger	Passenger complaint

The assessors don't expect you to know the answer to every possible scenario they introduce. They simply want to see how you react in challenging situations. So, when taking part in any role play scenario, use the following guidelines:

- Be proactive and do your best to resolve the situation using your initiative
- Remain calm and composed
- Be direct and assertive
- Immerse yourself into the role
- Take each scenario seriously
- Devise a plan and follow it as much as possible
- Have fun

Here are some pointers to help you deal with some common scenarios:

Passenger complaint

In the case of a passenger complaint, it is important that you listen to their concern without interruption. Ask questions, where appropriate, to clarify their concerns and show empathy towards their situation. If the facts warrant it, apologise for the situation, explain what action you intend to take and thank them for bringing the matter to your attention.

Scared passenger

If a passenger is fearful of flying, be considerate of their feelings. Use a gentle and calm tone to talk them through the flight and reassure them of any sounds or sensations they may experience. Let the passenger know where you can be found and show them the call bell.

Intoxicated passenger

Offer the passenger a cup of tea or coffee and don't provide any more alcoholic drinks. You could also encourage the passenger to eat some food. Remain calm towards the passenger, but be direct and assertive in your approach. If you feel it appropriate, inform your senior and seek assistance from other crewmembers.

CORPORATE CULTURE

As you already discovered in step one, corporate culture is a very important aspect that is always being assessed throughout your interactions and involvement in the group tasks. For this reason, you should always assume that no matter how irrelevant a task may appear, there is always an underlying motive for its inclusion, and you can almost always be sure it is being sized up against this important criteria.

Because each airline has a unique style, you will find that each selection process varies in its approach.

If you apply to one airline and find the interview process extremely challenging, it is possible that there is a mis-match with the corporate culture and you may find another selection process very easy and is exactly the reason they are carried out as they are.

So, don't be disheartened if you are having a challenge, you may simply need to adjust your focus or your approach.

On the following page are several breakdowns of the various airlines processes that I have experienced. Use these as guidelines to understand the approach, but be aware that the formats may change and may differ in different regions.

virgin atlantic

We began with a brief introduction given by the recruiters, followed by a quick round of mini self presentations about ourselves. The recruiters then handed each of us a card from which to read aloud to the group, this was very short and simple to read. We then carried out a reach test.

Next we were asked to network with the group, taking notes, and then present the information about what I learned about the candidates back to the group. During this task, recruiters picked out candidates for short one on one discussions.

Next we participated in a group discussion. This was based around creating a new advertising campaign for Virgin. We were handed a card with a song written on the back and asked to present our campaign to the tune of that song.

Then the first round of eliminations occured, with the remaining candidates participating in a series of very simple maths and psychometric tests. Any remaining candidates after this were sent to final interviews.

Emirates

Emirates also began with a brief introduction by the recruiters, alongside a short video presentation. Then the floor opened up to a question and answer session.

At the open day, there was a resume handover, but not at the inviatation only day. Several candidates were eliminated after the resume handover, so standing out and focusing on presentation was key when approaching the desk. Reach tests were also carried out at this stage.

After this, we participated in several group discussions, with eliminations taking place between each. We didn't do anything but discussion sessions.

We then filled out some very simple maths, English and apittude tests and had a mini discussion with the recruiter. Final interviews varied depending on the application method, I done mine at a later date, but many were done the next day.

BRITISH AIRWAYS

Before anything, British Airways will want to ensure you measure up, so expect to perform a reach test and have your height measured upon arrival. We also had to sit in a jump seat and demonstate our ability to fasten and unfasten a seatbelt.. Those who failed these tests were sent home.

Next the recruiters gave a short introduction about the airline, and then we were asked to participate in a multple choice question paper. These are all common sense, and very simple to complete.

Then we went through the various stages of the selection process. I had a group task first. then a role play scenario, and then the two on one interview. The role play lasted only a few minutes and was performed with the recruiter. During the final interview. I was also asked to read from a short scrpt.

As you can see, the approaches are quite different for each airline, and those approaches say a lot about what each airline values the most.

For Virgin, it was all about personality. flair and fun. Coincidentally, extroverted candidates faired well for Virgin.

Emirates were very much about communication. Many extroverted types were eliminated early, with the more introverted types being selected.

British Airways were very well rounded in their approach. covering all bases.

While these are just my observations, you can see that a candidate who may be unsuccessful at Virgin, may do very well at Emirates or BA. This is the corporate culture shining through and needs to be observed if you are to be successful and happy with your choice.

THE FINAL INTERVIEW

CONGRATULATIONS

Congratulations if you have made it through to the final interview. Having assessed your involvement and performance during the group sessions, the recruiters have clearly observed qualities in your character that they admire, and would now like to explore your motives further. So revel in the success you have achieved to this point, and be ready to close out this process.

During the final interview, the recruiters will seek to explore your motives for applying to the airline and your desire for pursuing a career as cabin crew. Moreover, they will seek to gather information about your work history, character and work ethic to determine whether you will fit the job and airline.

To ease you into the interview process, and make you feel more relaxed, the recruiters will typically open the session with questions about you and your background. They will then seek to explore your motivation for applying to the airline and making a career change. Questions such as "Why do you want to work for us?" and "Why do you want to be cabin crew?" are common at this stage.

With the interview thoroughly under way, the recruiters will want to determine whether you possess the skills and experience necessary for the position. Here you can expect more probing situational and behavioural questions, such as "When have you handled a customer complaint?" and "Describe a time when you failed to communicate effectively".

Although there appears to be no typical duration for panel interviews, you can expect a baseline time of at least 20 minutes, to upwards of 1 hour or more. In either case, the duration has no bearing on your ultimate success; so do not overly concern yourself with this aspect. An interview lasting just 20 minutes doesn't indicate a failure, just as an interview in excess of 1 hour does not indicate success.

WHAT RECRUITERS LOOK FOR

Recruiters understand that you will not be able to answer every question perfectly, and they also understand that you may not know the answer to each question that is asked. What they do expect and what they are interested in is how you respond to certain lines of questioning and how you conduct yourself. As such, their line of questioning will be designed to reveal your ability to:

- Listen actively
- Express yourself articulately, confidently and professionally
- Answer questions logically and concisely
- Remain calm under pressure

Some of the questions are designed specifically to throw you off guard, to see how you react to the pressure. With these sorts of questions, the interviewers are not necessarily looking for a perfect answer, but they are looking for a quick and well-prepared response.

Ultimately, it is important to remember that the recruiters are looking to hire positive people, so it is important to remain calm and composed throughout the interview and never show that you have been flustered.

AVOID FLAT ANSWERS

While it may make sense to memorise your answers, I would advise against this. Not only do you run the risk of sounding like a robot, with a boring and flat delivery, but you also risk forgetting your answers and appearing flustered as you try to recall the information.

Rather than memorising your answers, make a list of key points and try to remember those instead. Key points are much easier to remember and will allow you to create a genuine and spontaneous answer based around those key points.

Another technique, that is highly effective and advantageous, is to prepare through actual practice. Whether that is through a role play with a friend or family member, the use of a camcorder or through attending mock interviews with other airlines, practice will allow you to feel much more confident and natural when you do the real thing.

And remember to inject your personality as much as possible. Have stories at the ready and personal anecdotes because that is what will make you stand out and likeable, but also make you believable in your response.

Where people get lost is in not preparing at all and winging it, or over preparing and appearing static in their delivery. Take the middle ground. Just be yourself and be natural following the structures provided.

TRADITIONAL QUESTIONS

AS EASY AS A B C

When preparing your answers to traditional questions, keep the A.B.C formula in mind.

A = ANSWER

Make your answer concise by answering the question directly

B = BACK IT UP

Back up your answer with solid facts. This will add a lot of weight to any statements made.

C = CONCLUDE

The conclusion allows you to expand on your skills and what you can offer the airline

Consider the following example:

What is your best attribute?

> **ANSWER**
> "As you will have observed during the group assessments, I am a very welcoming and social individual who interacts well with others, and readily adapts to new people and environments."

> **BACK IT UP**
> "In fact, my previous supervisor also picked up on these attributes and often asked me to carry out the client shampoo because she knew I would make the clients feel welcome and relaxed"

> **CONCLUDE**
> "I am confident that this aspect of my character will enable me to perform the job to the same high standard that exists currently within the airline"

A C T ON NEGATIVE QUESTIONS

Negative questions can be better approached using the A.C.T formula

A = ATTACK

By attacking the question head on, not only do you avoid being alienated by the question, it also allows you to swiftly move on and sdd clarity to your response.

C = CLARIFY

This is your opportunity to add any clarity and facts that may support or justify your answer.

T = TURN

Now turn the focus away from the initial negative question to focus on the positive outcome of the experience.

Consider the following example:

What do you consider to be your greatest weakness?

> **ATTACK**
> "I recognise that my leadership ability is a potential area of improvement"

> **CLARIFY**
> "Which is why I am actively working on developing this area further through a part time training course at my local college"

> **TURN**
> "Although I am still learning, I see constant improvement in my capabilities when being faced with leadership tasks and I am confident that I will continue to learn and grow with experience"

PROBING QUESTIONS

Follow up questions are either used to verity the viability of your answer, or to tempt negative information into the open. So it is important to have examples ready to back up any statements made.

Prepare to be asked:

- What did you learn from the experience?
- What specifically did you say?
- How did you feel?
- Would you do anything differently?
- How did they react?
- What other options did you consider?
- Why did you decide to take the action that you did?
- You mentioned ... Tell me more about that.
- How did you retain your composure?
- Can you give me an example of that?
- Can you be more specific about...?

SAMPLE ANSWERS

TO THE TOP 10 MOST FREQUENTLY ASKED TRADITIONAL QUESTIONS

Tell me a little bit about yourself

> This question is usually asked early as an ice breaker. There is no need to delve into your childhood leisure pursuits here, the recruiters simply want a paraphrased overview of what you do, why you are attending the interview and what you have to offer. Show your personality because they want to learn more about you as a person, not simply a rehash of your resume.

"I currently work as a freelance hair consultant, and have worked in client-facing roles for the past eight years. During this time, I have worked my way up from a receptionist to a senior hair stylist, while simultaneously studying for my NVQ levels 1, 2 and 3.

While I very much enjoy the work I do, I'd love the chance to transfer the skills and experiences I have learnt to work as cabin crew, which is why I'm so excited about this opportunity with Fly High Airlines.

Even back as far as being a child, I have always wanted to become cabin crew and, during the course of my career, I have been gradually mastering the skills needed to perform its tasks. I'd now like to discuss how I might contribute to the ongoing success of Fly High Airlines by joining your team."

Tell me a little bit about yourself

Answer:

Why do you want to become cabin crew?

> An honest and passionate response to this question will surely set you apart. Think about it, why do you really want the job? Where did the desire come from? Was it a childhood dream, or was it sparked by another interest? Let your personality shine.

"For me, it's not just the job, but the whole lifestyle that interests me. On a personal note, I love the buzz of the airport because to me it represents action. The sense of satisfaction that everyone has a story and everyone is going somewhere for a reason sets off the excitement and motivation in me.

On a professional note, however, being a representative of the Fly High brand and being a part of the aviation industry are factors which draw me. Just being in the thick of things, in amongst the passengers where I can contribute to their entire experience is a major draw.

But ultimately, I want the job because I know I will be good at it. Not only would I positively thrive on the challenges of the position, but I have also built up a solid set of skills that will enable me to truly excel within the role.

Being cabin crew with Fly High Airlines really encapsulates everything that I want in a long term career and I can't think of anything I'd rather do."

Why do you want to become cabin crew?

Answer:

Why should we hire you?

> This is the time to shine, so don't be modest. Consider the experience and character traits that are most relevant and transferable to the position and explain how you have demonstrated these in the past.

> ANSWER
"Honestly, I feel as thought this job description was written with me in mind. I have worked in client facing roles for the past eight years so I am certainly qualified to perform the diverse requirements of this role but, beyond this, my character is tailored to this role.

> BACK IT UP
As you will have observed during the group assessments, I am a very welcoming and social individual who interacts well with others. I readily adapt to new people and environments and I can work alongside others as part of a unified team.

> CONCLUDE
These are all skills and qualities I will bring to the position and I am confident that these aspects of my personality and experience will enable me to perform the job to the same high standard that exists currently."

Why should we hire you?

Answer:

Back it up:

Conclude:

Why do you want to work for this airline?

> To make the greatest impact, begin with a personal story, but close with a demonstration of your knowledge and fit for the airline. This will make you stand out as an informed and enthusiastic individual who has something more to offer.

"Well, it actually goes back to my very first flight. I was finally earning enough to take my dream trip to Los Angeles and chose to fly with Fly High Airlines. Once on board, your crew did everything to make my flight the most memorable experience, and it has never been matched.

Once they had completed their crew duties, two of the crew offered to take me for a tour around the aircraft and into the flight deck to meet the pilots. Later into the flight, I had fallen asleep and missed the meals, but woke from my nap to find my tray table down and there were 3 chocolates on top of a hand written note which read "from your Fly High crew". Clearly this isn't part of the job description, so I was really impressed with the extra effort they had extended to me on my maiden voyage.

With this as a first experience, the bar has been set high and I've not encountered any experience like it, neither have I met such a dedicated and enthusiastic crew. I have also met many more Fly High crew who have worked for the airline for several years and still speak lovingly about their job and the airline. This, to me, is a clear testament of the Fly High brand and the quality of training you provide.

I would be honoured to work for and represent the Fly High brand and pass on that same smile I was awarded to another passenger."

Why do you want to work for this airline?

Answer:

What are your best qualities?

> Don't be shy, give it all you got. But, be sure to back it up with examples, ideally one which relates to the position if you have one.

> **ANSWER**
> This is a tough one to answer, but I'm going to say enthusiasm. Whatever happens in my life and no matter how bad things get, I am always able to see the postive aspects and keep a calm head. I think this has come from all the Tony Robbins videos I have watched.

> **BACK IT UP**
> I remember during my degree, I used to post little pep talk messages on the private group forum whenever I felt excited. The more I was struggling with an aspect of the course, the more positive and frequent my messages became. Often I would have a message from another student telling me how my message had come at the right time and it had put a smile on their face.

> **CONCLUDE**
> Not only does it help me remain postive and focused, but I get a huge sense of satisfaction when I am able to impart that enthusiasm onto others.

What are your best qualities?

Answer:

Back it up:

Conclude:

What is your greatest weakness?

> The key to answering questions about weaknesses is to focus your response on those skills you are actively learning or planning to develop. This could be assertiveness or leadership. The point is, it is only a weakness because you haven't yet mastered it, and that is why you are working on developing those skills further. Avoid weaknesses that are an integral part of the position.

> **ATTACK**
> Well, such is the joy of life, my greatest strength is also my greatest weakness. In being enthusiastic, I have learnt that not everyone is in tune or on that same level and doesn't necessarily want to be.

> **CLARIFY**
> I am learning to develop my awareness skills to understand when my enthusiasm is appropriate, and when it needs to be reigned in slightly.

> **TURN**
> It's taking some conscious effort to reign myself in, and I'm at the stage where my brain feels fried, but I'm getting better the more I practice, and I'm recieving positive feedback. I'm confident that I can get those skills where I need them to be and I see it as a good opportunity to develop my people sills further.

What is your greatest weakness?

Attack:

Clarify:

Turn:

What qualities do you think are necessary for cabin crew?

> The recruiters want to know that you understand what the role involves and what qualities are necessary to perform its tasks. Conclude this answer by acknowledging your skills in relation to the position.

"Cabin crew play a vital role in giving a good impression of the airline as a whole. This means crew members need to have good communication and customer care skills, as well as a friendly and welcoming demeanour, at all times and without exception.

Because of the importance of safety, it is also important that they have the strength of character to cope with difficult people and situations, in a calm and objective manner. It is also important that crew are respected as an authority if they are to be listened to and taken seriously, so an inner confidence, a sense of leadership and ability to be assertive are also essential skills.

Incidentally, these are all attributes I have, and are the primary reasons I would complement your existing team."

What qualities do you think are necessary for cabin crew?

Answer:

Why did you leave your last job?

> While you do need to be honest about your reasons for leaving past employment, you need to be diplomatic in your response. Being bored or not getting along with your boss are not ideal answers here.

No opportunities
"While I enjoyed working for my previous employer, and appreciate the skills I developed while I was there, I felt I was not being challenged enough in the job. After working my way up through the company, there were no further opportunities for advancement."

Redundancy
"I survived the first layoffs, but unfortunately this one got me."

Temporary position
"The job was only a temporary position which I took to broaden my experience."

Why did you leave your last job?

Answer:

What do you know about our airline?

> This is where your research will pay off handsomely. So, demonstrate your enthusiasm by sharing knowledge that will reveal the effort you have taken to learn more about the airline and its operations.

"Fly High Airlines began operating in 1980 with a single leased aircraft, serving just two destinations. The airline now serves 73 destinations in 48 countries worldwide and is rapidly expanding its route network, which is soon to include Colorado and Ohio.

From my personal experience of being a passenger, I also discovered that the 250 international awards for customer service excellence are certainly deserved as I have always found the most welcoming and enthusiastic crew on board my flights with Fly High Airlines.

I also note during my research that Conde Nast have quoted the airline to be the fastest growing and have said that Fly high is the airline to watch out for in taking the number one spot this year."

What do you know about our airline?

Answer:

What do you dislike about your current job?

> There will always be less than exciting aspects of a job, however, being critical about your job isn't going to create a positive impression. So, soften these aspects as much as possible and try to select neutral examples, such as paperwork, lack of job security or opportunities for growth.

"I honestly can't think of any major dislikes. I don't think I'd be able to really excel if I weren't truly interested in the work, or if I were merely motivated by its financial rewards. I guess my answer will have to come under the category of nuisances.

The biggest nuisance is the paperwork. I realise the importance of documentation, and I cooperatively fill out the forms, but I'm always looking for efficiencies in that area that will get me out in front of the client where I belong."

What do you dislike about your current job?

Answer:

BEHAVIOURAL QUESTIONS

The majority of the questioning will focus almost exclusively on personal qualities and behavioural questions. With this type of questioning there are no right or wrong answers, just more appropriate answers and better forms of expression.

The reason for this style of interview is because how you have applied certain skills and behaved in the past is often a clear indication of how you will behave in the future. In essence, the interviewers are looking to predict your future performance and determine if you have the qualities required to perform the duties of the role.

The key to preparing for this type of interview is to work with the job description and person specification that we covered in step one. All you need to do is tailor your answers to match and demonstrate those competencies.

Because you won't know what questions will be asked, it is important to enter the process with 3-5 short stories that highlight the most important core competencies. At the bare minimum, try to have an example for each of the following

> **TEAM SPIRIT**
>
> **CUSTOMER SERVICE**
>
> **COMMUNICATION**
>
> **CHALLENGING EXPERIENCE**

You can expect questions to similar to the following:

- Tell us about a time when you went out of your way to help a customer
- When could your customer service have been better?
- When have you solved a customer problem?
- Have you been confronted by an angry customer before?
- Tell me about a time when you have worked well within a team
- Have you ever struggled to fit in with your team mates?
- Tell me about a disagreement you have had with your colleagues
- Tell me about a problem you have faced and the steps you took to overcome it.

THE SARR FORMULA

When preparing your examples to competency-based questions, the S.A.R.R formula can help you structure your response.

S = SITUATION

Briefly describe the challenge, problem, or task

A = ACTION

Describe what you did and how you did it

R = RESULT

Describe the outcome and how your actions affected the outcome or the people involved

R = REFLECTION

Elaborate on what you learned from the experience and whether you would do things differently in the future.

Consider the following example:

When have you used your initiative to solve a problem?

> **SITUATION**
> "I was in the staff room during my lunch break, and I could hear a lot of noise coming from inside the salon. I went to investigate and two, very bored, little girls confronted me. I could sense that their excitement was causing a disruption and inconvenience"

> **ACTION**
> "I immediately took the initiative and attempted to occupy them by offering to plait their hair while they made bracelets from some hair beads. Their eyes sparkled with excitement and I was able to keep them occupied for the remainder of their visit"

> **RESULT**
> "We had lots of fun and, while the calm was restored, the stylist was able to complete their mothers' treatment"

> **REFLECTION**
> "I felt really pleased that with just a little extra effort, I had made such a big difference"

ANTICIPATE QUESTIONS

Your résumé is a very powerful document because it will influence the nature and direction of the interview to a great extent. The recruiters have no information about you beyond this piece of paper, so they will use it to formulate suitable questions. This allows an element of predictability, therefore giving you back some control.

Take a look through your resume and consider what questions may arise from what you have included. For example:

- If you have been self employed for some time, this could pose concerns about your ability to return to employment
- If you have large gaps in your employment or are currently unemployed, what are the reasons for those?
- Do you have only a short career history? or maybe you are going through a big career change, for what reason have you decided to change career paths?

Also take time to consider questions what may be relevant specifically to the airline or the position

» If the position involves a relocation, you may be asked about your knowledge of the location being transferred to.
» If there is a cultural element, you may be asked questions about your knowledge there also.
» And what about the challenges of the position. You'll most certainly want to know how you'll cope with the demands of the job

You don't need to have a solid answer for every single thing, but you should give some thought to anything that is obvious.

When I was being interviewed for Emirates, I was asked about my knowledge of Dubai and how I would cope with the transition to living within a Muslim country.

When being interviewed for CrossAir, my history of self employment was brought up as a concern, as was my willingness ot relocate to Switzerland. They even asked if I would miss my family and how I would feel to miss out on special family occassions.

Think ahead.

ACTION STEP

Write out a list of questions you expect to be asked about your particular circumstances
Think about your answers and make 2-3 key points for each.

POSSIBLE QUESTIONS

ASKING QUESTIONS

This section of the interview is a real chance for you to shine and set yourself apart from all the other candidates. Therefore, it is a good idea to prepare one or two intelligent questions in advance.

The questions you ask, and how you ask them, say a lot about you, your motives, your depth of knowledge about the airline and the position itself.

Guidelines

The questions you ask should follow these guidelines:

» Don't ask questions that could be easily answered through your own research.
» Ask questions which demonstrate a genuine interest in and knowledge of the airline and the position.
» Demonstrate that you know just that little bit more than is required.

Question About Suitability

Asking recruiters to raise their concerns about your suitability will provide you with an opportunity to follow up and reassure the recruiter.

- Do you have any reservations about my ability to do this job?
- What do you foresee as possible obstacles or problems I might have?
- Is there anything else I need to do to maximise my chances of getting this job?
- How does my background compare with others you have interviewed?
- Is there anything else you'd like to know?
- What do you think are my strongest assets and possible weaknesses?
- Do you have any concerns that I need to clear up in order to be a considered candidate?

Questions About the Recruiter

Asking recruiters about their views and experience in the job or working with the airline will demonstrate your genuine interest and motives.

- How did you find the transition in relocating to …?
- Why did you choose to work at … airlines?
- What is it about this airline that keeps you working here?
- It sounds as if you really enjoy working here, what have you enjoyed most about working for … airlines?

General Questions

» How would you describe the company culture?
» I feel my background and experience are a good fit for this position, and I am very interested. What is the next step?

No Questions

» I did have plenty of questions, but we've covered them all during our discussions. I was particularly interested in ... but we've dealt with that thoroughly.
» I had many questions, but you've answered them all you have been so helpful. I'm even more excited about this opportunity than when I applied.

Questions to Avoid

You should avoid asking questions such as those following as they will make you appear selfishly motivated.

» How many day's holiday allowances will I receive?
» What is the salary?
» When will I receive a pay increase?
» How many free flights will my family receive?
» Can I request flights to ...?

PAGE 247

STEP FIVE
CONCLUDE
... and you've made it

WOO HOO

You've made it through the enitre interview process, you've navigated your way through the gorup interview and woo'd the interviewers with your answers during the final interivew, and now comes the hardest part of all. Waiting for the **golden call.**

I kid you not, this is tough and weeks will feel like years as you await to discover your fate.

Hopefully this final step will help to get you through it, although I'm not sure anything can help beyond getting the phone to ring. But here goes, let's do this.

JOURNAL THE EXPERIENCE

During this step five, all I want you to do is take some time to write a short journal of what happened during your recruetement experience.

Journaling will achieve two very important things:

> **1. Get it out of your system**

Whatever has happened, you're not going to stop thinking and analysing it to death, so you might as well go full steam ahead and write it all out. Get it out of your head and onto paper so that you can at least start to make some sense out of everytihng. It may even help you feel more relaxed.

> **2. Give you a reference point for the future**

The second and, most important, reason for journaling is that there is a chance that the conditions weren't right for you on this particular occasion and it will help you immensely if you keep a log of your expeirence to help you prepare for the next opportunity.

As time goes on, you begin to forget what you could have improved upon or what you learnt, so journalling soon after the interview is over while they are fresh in your mind will lead you towards being successful later on. Remember to be as objective as possible for best results.

Date:

Airline:

What went well?:

What could I have improved upon?:

How was my mood before the interview? Was I relaxed?

How much sleep did I have? Did I feel rested?

How many people were present?

Did I smile? How was my demeanour?

Did I achieve rapport with the interviewer? How was my eye contact?

Any other points to note:

Any other points to note:

It's time to go out there and

live your dream

Please share your thoughts

If you found this book informative and helpful, please take a moment to review it online. Your review helps other people find this book and be helped by it's guidance also. I appreciate every review!

I love hearing your experiences and successes

Thank you for putting your faith in me to help you achieve your dreams. I hope to hear of your success soon.

Caitlyn Rogers xo

Introducing DreamCurves

The curve friendly

BODY SHAPING & RECOMPOSITION PROGRAM

Designed exclusively for women

CPSIA information can be obtained
at www.ICGtesting.com
Printed in the USA
BVHW021259030119
536900BV00011BA/215/P